Epilogue

Books by Frederick Morgan

POETRY

The One Abiding, 2003
The Night Sky,
with photographs by Gaylen Morgan, 2002
Poems for Paula, 1995
Poems: New and Selected, 1987
Eleven Poems, 1983
Northbook, 1982
Refractions, 1981
Seven Poems by Mallarmé,
with images by Christopher Wilmarth, 1981
The River, 1980
Death Mother and Other Poems, 1979
Poems of the Two Worlds, 1977
A Book of Change, 1972

PROSE

The Fountain and Other Fables, 1985
The Tarot of Cornelius Agrippa, 1978

EDITOR

The Modern Image, 1965
The Hudson Review Anthology, 1961

Epilogue

Selected and Last Poems

❧

FREDERICK MORGAN

Edited by

PAULA DEITZ

Red Hen Press | *Pasadena, CA*

Book layout by Jared Paul Burton & Isiah Lyons

Library of Congress Cataloging-in-Publication Data

Names: Morgan, Frederick, 1922–2004, author. | Deitz, Paula, editor.
Title: Epilogue: selected and last poems / Frederick Morgan ; edited by
  Paula Deitz.
Description: Pasadena, CA: Red Hen Press, [2022]
Identifiers: LCCN 2021046232 (print) | LCCN 2021046233 (ebook) | ISBN
  9781636280424 (trade paperback) | ISBN 9781636280431 (epub)
Subjects: LCGFT: Poetry.
Classification: LCC PS3563.O83 E65 2022 (print) | LCC PS3563.O83 (ebook)
  | DDC 811/.54—dc23/eng/20211006
LC record available at https://lccn.loc.gov/2021046232
LC ebook record available at https://lccn.loc.gov/2021046233

Publication of this book has been made possible in part through the generous financial support of Dana and Mary Gioia.

The National Endowment for the Arts, the Los Angeles County Arts Commission, the Ahmanson Foundation, the Dwight Stuart Youth Fund, the Max Factor Family Foundation, the Pasadena Tournament of Roses Foundation, the Pasadena Arts & Culture Commission and the City of Pasadena Cultural Affairs Division, the City of Los Angeles Department of Cultural Affairs, the Audrey & Sydney Irmas Charitable Foundation, the Meta & George Rosenberg Foundation, the Albert and Elaine Borchard Foundation, the Adams Family Foundation, Amazon Literary Partnership, the Sam Francis Foundation, and the Mara W. Breech Foundation partially support Red Hen Press.

First Edition
Published by Red Hen Press
www.redhen.org

Contents

DEATH MOTHER AND OTHER POEMS
(1979)

REFRACTIONS &
SEVEN POEMS BY MALLARMÉ
(1981)

from
NORTHBOOK
(1982)

I

THE ONE ABIDING
(2003)

I

II

III

IV

LAST POEMS

Epilogue

A Being in Time: On the Poetry of Frederick Morgan

Through how many lives have I traveled,
in how many shapes found my being?

—"The Priest"

An answer may be given, it seems,
before the question's asked—
a pause outside of time precede
the immutable unwindings.
Death, too, is there with its meaning
before a life begins.

—"I love grim autumn days . . ."

Frederick Morgan—best known as a founder of *The Hudson Review* and
for fifty years its leading editor—was a civilized man in the classical sense,
accepting of the body for its beauty and mortality, alert to the natural world,
skeptical of human ambitions. The magazine he edited has held a central
place in American letters since 1948, publishing T. S. Eliot, Ezra Pound,
Wallace Stevens, William Carlos Williams, Thomas Mann, Theodore
Roethke, Eudora Welty, Elizabeth Bishop, and Sylvia Plath. It introduced
and supported such writers as W. S. Merwin, Anthony Hecht, Louis
Simpson, A. R. Ammons, William Stafford, Rhina P. Espaillat and Anne
Sexton, not to mention figures in my own generation including Dana Gioia,
Emily Grosholz, A. E. Stallings and Charles Martin. A literary review in the
best tradition, it surveys the worlds of fine art and dance and cinema as well
as literature. For generations now, the review has cultivated strong writing—
often scrappy and vital, independent, never beholden to academic or
literary fashion. It has published fiction and travel writing, translations and
essays. Frederick Morgan was also himself a marvelous poet, one who

developed late his own voice, often finding power in restraint, yet sometimes remarkably liberated. The importance of his poetry derives not only from increasing technical facility, but also from what it captures and preserves of the man himself—a breadth of thought and experience triumphing over suffering and loss, rooted in stoicism but, especially in his love poems, moving through it to fulfillment and joy. The editor whose rigorous openness created a crucial magazine is also the man who found his way as an artist. He left a body of work that rewards readers with its unusual lucidity, simplicity, and wisdom—rather like being in the presence of the man himself.

I have many fond memories of that presence. I first wrote for *The Hudson Review* in 1991 and spoke on the phone with Fred just a month or so before his death in early 2004. Others of my generation who knew him longer have pointed out that his late start as a poet (he published his first book in 1972 at age fifty) made him both our elder and our contemporary. He developed as a writer alongside younger poets, so he seemed a comrade-in-arms as much as a father figure. The man who in an interview could refer to Ezra Pound as "a real pain in the ass," and to "the excitement of discovering Anne Sexton's first poems," was utterly unpretentious in his authority. But the authority was undeniable, every bit as much as the trust he gave to younger writers, allowing us to develop and make our own mistakes.

Once he visited a class I was teaching at the West Chester Poetry Conference in Pennsylvania. I was discussing a lyric poem in idealistic terms, saying the poet "wrote like an angel," and Fred gently demurred: "Why would he want to write like an angel? Why not a human being, an ordinary man?" It was a difference in poetics between the poet in question and the older man seated calmly before me, and I sensed that these theoretical poles were more familiar to him than to me. Morgan's poetic is that of an ordinary man, albeit a thoughtful and cultivated one, among other things a body in time. In one of his best short poems, "The Master," which appeared in *Northbook*, his fourth collection of original poems (1982), Morgan seems to be clarifying his poetic:

> When Han Kan was summoned
> to the imperial capital
> it was suggested he sit at the feet of
> the illustrious senior court painter
> to learn from him the refinements of the art.

"No, thank you," he replied,
"I shall apprentice myself to the stables."

And he installed himself and his brushes amid the dung and the flies,
and studied the horses—their bodies' keen alertness—
eye-sparkle of one, another's sensitive stance,
the way a third moved graceful in his bulk—

and painted at last the emperor's favorite,
the charger named "Nightshining White,"
whose likeness after centuries still dazzles.

Morgan's own generation of poets often represented Asian poetry in simple diction and in free verse like this, so the artistry of the poem is subdued to its subject. But this is not a translation. It is an homage, respectful of manner. The parable's simplicity leaves open the question of artistry itself, mastery itself—whether art or life or both are at stake.

In this regard, I think also of Morgan's fine translation of Baudelaire's "A Voyage to Cythera," which ends:

On your isle, Venus, I saw but one thing standing,
gallows-emblem from which my shape was hanging...
God! Give me strength and will to contemplate
heart, body—without loathing, without hate.

Morgan had known all the dark emotions that Baudelaire relishes and resists, and the poems indicate that he was unafraid of them. But from the start he saw them in perspective. He had known more suffering than many people experience in a lifetime. His first wife died of her addiction to alcohol, and three of his six children predeceased him—one by suicide, one of illness, one in a drug-addled motorcycle wreck. While he is rarely explicit about these events, they underlie not only his moments of despair, but also the progress of the body through time and toward acceptance and love. There is a great story behind these poems—the story of a man letting go of any need for redemption and finding instead the practice and equanimity of a master. The story is related through many genres and forms—narrative, meditative, lyric, and dramatic—but the sensibility behind every poem is the same being in time, the same extraordinary man.

The best essay yet written about this poetry is by Dana Gioia, one of those "younger poets" who thought of Morgan as their contemporary. "The Three Lives of Frederick Morgan" was first delivered as a lecture at the University of the South, where a number of us had gathered to honor Fred as he received the Aiken Taylor Award for Modern American Poetry. Gioia's essay is significant for two reasons: its lucid vision of three voices in the poems (child, lover and philosopher), and the fact that Morgan's work was being described not by one of his own contemporaries, who often knew him best as an editor, but by a younger writer who felt a close connection to the poetry. Gioia laments that critics had not yet come to terms with Morgan's poetry because of its "ambidexterity" and formal variety: "Morgan's poetry reveals a complete independence from the aesthetic and ideological conflicts that have typified American poetry over the past thirty years. . . . He must be evaluated on his own terms—or not at all." Gioia's knack for celebrating artistic eccentricity suits the reading of this work, which is sometimes less notable for its style than its content, while at the same time being utterly free of ideological agendas. The poetry is, as I have said, fully expressive of a remarkable man, and it stands on its own in the literary landscape.

Born into a wealthy New York family on April 25, 1922, Morgan was raised an only child in a household where neither parents nor servants kept him from a "pervasive feeling of loneliness," as he told William Baer in an interview. "I was a solitary child surrounded by older people; and although I had opportunities to play with other children in both the city and the country, I still spent a great deal of time alone. As a result, I did a lot of reading. I was able to read at a very early age, and I read a tremendous amount of children's literature, especially fairy tales and fantasies of various kinds. So I had a highly developed interior life along with an undeveloped social life, which seems to have worked both ways. . . . So I think that's the source of that particular image in my poetry—which no one has ever commented on before except my friend Emily Grosholz who once said, 'You know, you're always looking out the window.'"

While not an uncommon experience for a writer, these ruminations do illuminate Morgan's particular poetic. The child is important in his work because it is an essential consciousness of being alive in the world, and while the narrative arc of the whole oeuvre involves a man becoming, in a sense, the hero of his own life, that essential child's vision is never entirely lost to the being in time. Morgan had been working as the editor of *The Hudson Review* for twenty years before two events jolted him back into writing poetry—the suicide of his son John in 1968 and his marriage to Paula

Deitz, who became a muse and the great love of his life, the following year. Morgan's first collection, *A Book of Change* (1972), reveals many of these obsessions already in place. Gioia suggests that the book "is very much a beginner's volume—clear, heartfelt, well-shaped, but often under-realized. It is the work of a mature mind but not yet a mature poet." This may be true, but several poems stand out for their acute observations of life. Here is "Scotch Mary":

> Scotch Mary lived in the kitchen with the *News*.
> I was afraid of her. She wore old, broken shoes,
> was huge and shapeless, her hair in a frowsy bun.
> Often she chased me out of the kitchen fast
> but sometimes let me sit at the zinc-topped table
> where she drank her coffee with the pages outspread
> and read about rich people and the bad things they did.
>
> One summer afternoon the ceiling fell
> somewhere in the back. A great crash. I cried out,
> not thinking, "Mary! Where's Mary?" No one was hurt,
> but she came from her little room and held me tight
> against her until I gasped. "God bless the child!
> He thought of old Mary, he thought of old Mary," she said.

Like a scene from a novel, the poem reveals dawning awareness of social class and complex sympathies for other people. It's no wonder that as an editor Morgan would be so responsive to the revival of narrative poetry in the 1980s. This moment in time, this effort to recapture lost time in order to understand it, is also characteristic of many poems throughout Morgan's career, including his late masterpiece "Washington Square."

Another early poem, "Sometimes I hear...," evokes the losses that had hurt him into verse and the shocks forcing him to explore his own identity as a man: "Sometimes I hear my father's voice, sometimes my son's, in mine: / the modulations of two who have moved / beyond these tides of being. Dead and gone..."

Yet another aspect of Morgan's explorations of mortality in the poems is his frank enjoyment of sex. "The Oppositions," for example, uses the familiar image of Odysseus to express our pagan connections to nature, to the gods, to what is in us and beyond us at the same time: "Does it come to the same thing, then—all this strong journeying, / and lassitude of passive bodies in the hot noon sun? / If Odysseus remains, the god is in the fucking; / if he leaves, it is the god within who moves him on." If, when reading Morgan's poems of childhood, I think of Hardy's "The Self-Unseeing" with its ironic nostalgia, his poems about love and sex suggest the work of D. H. Lawrence and Robert Graves—the latter a poet Morgan published in the *Review*.

One early poem pointing toward the work of Morgan's maturity is "The Way," which concludes,

> Above all, do not use man to help out heaven
> or your mind, to help out what you cannot know.
>
> Be yourself, as an old misshapen tree
> is itself whether living or dead or beyond life and death.
>
> Then you may move among the myriads
> invulnerable, and play your part as well.

As in poets like Yeats (a Morgan favorite), one feels the writing bound up in the drama of the life—not as simple confessionalism, if such a thing exists, but as a struggle for self-realization. Art might not be, in Auden's phrase, "a midwife to society," but it is wrought in the birth pangs of the individual soul.

Morgan's second collection, *Poems of the Two Worlds* (1977), is an advance on the first, partly in its formal range, from lyrics to sequences, which would become a favorite mode. "When it rained and rained . . ." shows us the child poet looking out of windows, as Grosholz observed is so often the case. "Memories" is a sequence partly about the poet's sexual history, while "Exotica" offers epigrammatic poems owing something to *The Greek Anthology*. Morgan had received a strong literary education at Princeton, where his most influential teacher was Allen Tate. It was Tate, in fact, who convinced Morgan and his friend Joseph Bennett to found a magazine. After the war, in which Morgan served in the Army's Tank Destroyer Corps (his poor eyesight kept him Stateside and out of combat), he visited Ezra Pound at St. Elizabeths Hospital. He had studied the French Symbolists and felt sympathy with the erudition of the High Modernists, but he never shared their social snobbery. Steeped in classical literature, he would also admit to relishing genre fiction, pulp novels, science fiction and whodunnits. The sensibility we begin to see in the poems is both learned and earthy—a modern man in search of a soul, capable of letting the poem's drama exist outside his own. Here is "Bones":

The bones go under the soil, under the soil
at year's end the bones go under the soil—
sometimes they wave red flags
sometimes they speak not at all

The bones are boats that go sailing in the black ground
clean through the earth and out the other side
in an everyday kind of way
into the sun again

The bones speak to the birds, the birds sing back
but the language is lost before it comes to the ears
of fools who run to and fro
between the birds and the bones

I killed a fool once and drank blood from his skull
and taking his bony fingers in my hand
asked him where he expected to go:
he didn't say yes, he didn't say no

Bones have a home underground or so I'm told.
They are themselves the city in which they dwell
and have a meaning, too, since they once were we:
another meaning is coming, wait and see

This poem is less conceptualized than some of Morgan's early work, more open to the promptings of language itself. It foreshadows some of his freest later writing.

In two long sequences, "Poems of the Two Worlds" and "Blue Hill Poems," Morgan reveals an awareness of mystical thinking and what would become sophisticated underpinnings of Buddhism: "After breakfast, God takes his random walk / in the cool glades where nothingness has being: / his thoughts rejoin themselves beneath the trees." The poems comprehend a *via negativa* helping the poet objectify his personal crises:

Somewhere, in an antiworld,
a man has risen and looks out from his window;
his face is mine, but if we should shake hands
all worlds, thoughts, gods would find their fiery end,

being reduced to your simplicity,
God, who are Any, All, and None—in one.
Now, please, retire; and claws be sheathed.
Cold and bright the day's begun.

The personal crises would not soon abate but would be tempered by joy in his life with Paula, his third wife, his partner in editing the magazine and his muse. But in these early poems and sequences, the effort to find philosophical equilibrium predominates. "Being is known only / by being itself, in its own dimension—" he writes in "Blue Hill Poems." ". . . yes, eyes are holes in the world's face, through which something else / does its own huge seeing." Eyes and windows, interior and exterior situations of being—these are the themes Grosholz noticed so precisely. She writes of them in her introduction to *The Night Sky* (2002), a beautiful late book of Morgan's poems illustrated with photographs by his daughter, Gaylen. The book, Grosholz says, "meditates on the theme of transitions, of thresholds. Its topics are the demise of imperfect loves, the destruction of old orders, the destabilizing power inherent in eros as well as in language itself; and its locations . . . are the littoral (between earth and sea), the graveyard (between life and death), and the dream (between waking and sleep)." The flowering of Morgan's later poetry, the discovery of more flexible and ecstatic forms of expression, would become his major contribution as a writer.

Two personal memories anchor my sense of Fred Morgan's hard-won kindness and wisdom. The first has to do with my own mother's struggles with alcoholism—a battle she eventually won, achieving a serenity in her later years I had not dreamed possible. During one of the worst periods of her affliction, Fred wrote me, saying I shouldn't feel alone in my situation, that every family had difficulties like these. He did not mention his own first wife's alcoholism or his son Seth's battles with addiction—battles terribly lost.

The second memory has to do with my father's Alzheimer's disease, and my then-mother-in-law's suffering from the same devastating illness while she lived with my wife and me in Colorado. On a warm summer evening, I was sitting with Fred and Paula during a picnic at the West Chester Poetry Conference. Fred always wanted to know how his younger friends were doing. I must have been telling him about my terror of this disease, my fear that I was doomed to suffer it myself, that I had to get my writing done quickly because I might not have brains enough to finish my life's work. I was agitated and depressed. Fred listened quietly, then with gentle firmness reached across the table and took hold of my hand. Looking directly into my eyes, he said, "Dave, you can't live that way."

It was one of the simplest gifts I have ever been given by another person—a gesture of fatherhood and friendship—and for a time I felt as if a great weight had been lifted off my shoulders. Fred knew the drama of becoming adult in the truest sense, facing death, taking responsibility for one's own life, accepting joy where one finds it. His classical training in stoicism and his interest in Buddhism were part of it, but so was the fact of his own suffering and his own knowledge of joy. This is the struggle of both the life and the poems, and it animates the superb work in his third collection, *Death Mother and Other Poems* (1979).

Reviewing the book in *The Southern Review*, Dana Gioia announced with characteristic wit, "At the age of fifty-eight, Frederick Morgan has become one of the most interesting young poets in America." The youthful vitality of Morgan's later work connects him in some ways to Yeats, as does the fascination with mysticism and sex. *Death Mother* is the book in which Morgan grapples openly with the fatal alcoholism of his first wife in poems like "Canandaigua" and "We took a room at the Westbury . . ." And in one of his most beautiful poems, "February 11, 1977," he squarely faces the suicide of his son John:

> You died nine years ago today.
> I see you still sometimes in dreams
> in white track-shirt and shorts, running,
> against a drop of tropic green.
>
> It seems to be a meadow, lying
> open to early morning sun:
> no other person is in view,
> a quiet forest waits beyond.
>
> Why do you hurry? What's the need?
> Poor eager boy, why can't you see
> once and for all you've lost this race
> though you run for all eternity?
>
> Your youngest brother's passed you by
> at last: he's older now than you—
> and all our lives have ramified
> in meanings which you never knew.

And yet, your eyes still burn with joy,
your body's splendor never fades—
sometimes I seek to follow you
across the greenness, into the shade

of that great forest in whose depths
houses wait and lives are lived,
where you haste in gleeful search of me
bearing a message I must have—

but I, before I change, must bide
the "days of my appointed time,"
and so I age from self to self
while you await me, always young.

The persona of these personal poems has grown by facing facts and squeezing the last drops of sentimentality out of them. "But why not say what happened?" Robert Lowell had asked just a few years earlier when the melding of art and life seemed inevitable for a while.

But *Death Mother* is not a book that rests solely in the personal. As with all of his books, Morgan remains interested in history, mythology, philosophy and other ways of expanding the possibilities of his art. A poem like "The Touch" pulls together personal and impersonal elements in what you might call a statement of poetics, while "Orpheus to Eurydice" and the powerful title sequence explore the place of poetry in relation to death and love. In "The Trader," Morgan expands more fully into narrative, while "Three Children Looking over the Edge of the World" flirts with allegory:

They came to the end of the road
and there was a wall across it
of cut stone—not very high.

Two of them boosted the third up
between them, he scrambled to the top
and found it wide enough to sit on easily.
Then he leaned back and gave the others a hand.

One two three in a row they sat there
staring: there was no bottom.

Below them a cliff went down and down for ever

and across from them, facing them, was nothing—
an emptiness that had no other side
and turned their vision back upon itself.

So there wasn't much to do or look at, after all.
One of them told a rhyme, the others chimed in,
and after a little while they swung around and let themselves back down.

But when their feet touched solid road again
they saw at once they had dropped from the top of the sky
through sun and air and clouds and trees
and that the world was the wall.

The blunt realization of that ending reminds me of Anthony Hecht's "A Hill" with its Beckett-like bleakness. What if the world were the wall? What does their climbing and vision signify? And what happens to perspective in the poem? How is the vision of children like the vision of an aging man? Poems don't answer questions so much as pose them, and this one leaves me darkly beguiled.

In 1981, Morgan published two collections of translations, *Refractions* and *Seven Poems by Mallarmé*, arising from preoccupations of his university days. They allow us to see influences from the Greeks, the personal dramas of Catullus, the urbanity of Horace, and in general Morgan's debt to multiple literary traditions[1]. *Northbook* continues in this vein with a sequence based upon Norse mythology, then follows it with such fine poems as "Skulls," "The Master," and "The River," one of his most beautiful sequences. *Poems: New and Selected* (1987) began with a selection of new work, including "Meditations for Autumn," which would reappear in 2003 as "Meditation at Sundown." Under the new title, the poem bore the dedication "In memory of my son Seth"—he had died in 1990. Both versions of the poem contain these chilling lines:

---

1   Much more could be said about Fred's support of translation in *The Hudson Review* (as well as fiction and drama). One of the magazine's three co-founders was the classical translator William Arrowsmith, while Richmond Lattimore served on the board. Among the *Review's* earliest publications was Pound's translation of Sophokles' *Women of Trachis* as well as *The Analects of Confucius*.

> From the being born to the dying
> life is a butchery.
> The primitives got it right
> with their ritual compensations.
>
> For those more enlightened, however,
> the unacceptable lurks
> just beyond the visible circle—
> knife at the ready.

Indeed, the stench of life's carnage rarely completely leaves Morgan's poetry.

Yet in 1995 he published his most luminous book, *Poems for Paula*, a slender collection as simple and perfect as anything he wrote. Poems about joyful days at his summer home in Maine are followed by scenes from the couple's life in New York. We find him once again looking out a window in "The Breathing Space," but this time the window is open, and he is calling to his beloved on the street below. The breathing space is a brief realization of joy before the pain of recollection returns:

> That's why I'm grateful for those times
> when time itself comes to a stop
> on some quite ordinary day,
> comes to a stop for a random moment
>
> in which the self gains breathing space
> to find itself outside of time—
> as I've been found, who still hold fast
> that pause made radiant by her smile.

The poems are nearly artless in the best sense of that word, true to their emotions, simple, unmediated by literary calculation, yet delicately shaped.

When Fred's final volume, *The One Abiding*, appeared in 2003, with Gioia's essay for an introduction, it seemed a culminating event, encapsulating all the obsessions of his writing life with even greater finish to the poems, a few of which feel like Housman at his best—spare, down-to-earth, but evocative of complex feelings. The opening poem, "Washington Square," is the most sophisticated formal achievement of his career as well as an elegy for childhood friends. The poem concludes,

Comrades!—how has life served you all?
Benjy grew up a drunkard, Paul
was killed in Normandy, and Sue
moved somewhere west, was lost from view.
Sweet Laura, first to go,
died of the polio
in '33—my love, aged ten.
Sometimes I wish you back again,

the four of you, just as you were,
triumphant in that eager stir
of childhood—and myself with you
as I was then . . . But it won't do.
No dream of holding fast
to a beloved past
can cloud the heads of those who know
what's dead is dead, and rightly so.

Children still play in Washington Square
but they don't roam free, they must beware—
gone is their ancient liberty.
Gone, too, that civic decency
which cherished old and young
who shared the common tongue.
America bows to new, weak gods;
its children play against the odds.

Laura, Benjamin, Paul and Sue,
you've gone your ways. I'm going, too.
Our early joys were dearly bought—
the world was never what we thought—
and yet, we're justified:
it wasn't we who lied.
Now leave me, friends, and leaving, bless.
Once more I face the emptiness.

Recent history would hardly cause us to question this vision of childhood.
The book is mature in its mordancy. "May Night" is a dark love sonnet,

suggestive of betrayal, and several poems take up bloody classical subjects. One of the best is "Hypatia," which retells how a mob of Christians murdered the neo-Platonic philosopher, mathematician and astronomer. The poem's blunt closure underlines Morgan's tragic view of life:

> They burned all that was left of her—
> last of the great Plotinian line,
> Theon's daughter, Synesius' friend,
> humbled to dust by Coptic swine.
>
> The bishop who had egged them on,
> Cyril (later canonized),
> made known to all the outside world
> he was displeased, shocked, mortified
>
> by this excess of righteous zeal.
> Still, he kept safe his scurvy crew
> by bribing all the magistrates:
> he'd have more work for them to do . . .
>
> And that was it. Hypatia died.
> The old gods faded past recall.
> A new god triumphed—if new he was,
> and not the oldest one of all.

Other poems I find particularly affecting in this volume include "The Burial," "Nothing," and "Rain," which would have fit neatly in with *Poems for Paula*. The significance of its happiness is deepened by the darkness and violence of poems surrounding it.

A small group of "Last Poems" has now been added to Fred's oeuvre. Paula Deitz and I have gone over these previously uncollected poems, removing some we thought redundant or unfinished. What remains is good, sexy work—as if even more of the wildness of the later Yeats were set free in the writing. A frank example can be found in "Remember Waco":

> We felt around and kissed a while
> and said we liked each other's smell,
> and then I had you suck my cock—

you tensed at first, as if from shock,
then seemed to like it very well,
        remember?

It was the first time you'd done that,
you said, but showed how you were game
by setting to it with a will—
and so, I licked you too, until,
throbbing and quaking, we both came,
        remember?

The current puritanism that has descended on the country, people seeking justice everywhere but losing joy and spontaneity in the process, might cause some readers to turn these pages squeamishly. But there is life in them, faced as honestly as Morgan faces our mortality.

And mortality, our consciousness of being in and out of time, is precisely the subject that always held him. You can see it in his early poem "The Step," which would in its understated perfection have been worthy of his final book as well. The poem is also liminal, involving a door rather than a window. It is, like so much of Morgan's work, about transition and the presence of change:

From where you are at any moment you
may step off into death.
Is it not a clinching thought?
I do not mean a stoical bravado
of making the great decision blade in hand
but the awareness, all so simple, that
right in the middle of the day
you may be called to an adjoining room.

—David Mason

from

A BOOK OF CHANGE

(1972)

The soul lives by that which it loves rather than in the body
which it animates. For it has not its life in the body,
but rather gives it to the body and lives in that which it loves.
—ST. JOHN OF THE CROSS

The Valley Spirit never dies,
It is called the Mysterious Female,
and the doorway of the Mysterious Female
is the base from which Heaven and Earth spring.
It is there within us all the time.
Draw upon it as you will, it never runs dry.
—LAO TZU

Port Caradoc

Before the dawn men dream of shapes of ships;
the women beside them softly part their lips.
The children sleep—their sleep spreads deep beneath
cradle and house, where the sea-bottom heaves.
The houses crouch like cats in the dawn haze,
the cats roam, big as houses, on the hills
and in backyards ash cans by twos and threes
raise a loveless lament to the darkling breeze.

Brisk on the bay, the waves roll in bright-capped
to the brackish beach where kelp and shells are heaped.
The men with pails stroll downhill to the docks
in the brilliant air—their wives watch their slow backs—
and soon sharp echoes rise, quick-multiplied,
of mallets rapping from the harborside,
as the morning mists lift slowly in the heat
from chalky uplands strewn with stolid sheep.

High noon: the sun is bellowing like a bull.
He fills the womb with gold, with honey the skull,
and summer smells rise rampant from moist ground
where worms delve damply in their solemn rounds.
By white-fenced yards the warm bees dart and drone
and skim the face of the boy who naps alone
while the sun-drenched rose luxuriously distends
her fragrant cap to the wind's light finger-ends.

The supplest lovers couple after supper:
they grapple, happily, behind the chapel.
Others, less delicately tuned to lust,
chat on their porches in the purple dusk.
The children drowse apart, minds groping deep
along dim ocean floors where great crabs creep,
while father, mothers mutter in their beds . . .

Dreams of the wide sea brim their desperate heads.

Scotch Mary

Scotch Mary lived in the kitchen with the *News,*
I was afraid of her. She wore old, broken shoes,
was huge and shapeless, her hair in a frowsy bun.
Often she chased me out of the kitchen fast
but sometimes let me sit at the zinc-topped table
where she drank her coffee with the papers outspread
and read about rich people and the bad things they did.

One summer afternoon the ceiling fell
somewhere in the back. A great crash. I cried out,
not thinking, "Mary! Where's Mary?" No one was hurt,
but she came from her little room and held me tight
against her until I gasped. "God bless the child!
He thought of old Mary, he thought of old Mary," she said.

"Sometimes I hear ..."

Sometimes I hear my father's voice, sometimes my son's, in mine:
the modulations of two who have moved
beyond these tides of being. Dead and gone,

but still their shapes appear as though in sudden shafts of sun:
Dad in the corner at "39"
smoking his pipe; John standing at my desk

smiling, talking to me of school, or politics, or girls.
Both images are strong in me today,
more real than half the people whom I meet,

as if their being, somehow, is in very loss confirmed.
Reality may be enclosed in mind
for who knows at what point the mind has end?

The world that is not here may be a world of sun and trees,
a world of man's potentialities:
our absences may there be presences.

Perhaps, in the long run, all mind, all memory is shared,
just as the body's basic stuff is shared
that crumbles and renews, as time moves on

(dissembling time, whose circuit may be but one long day's dream!)
in other bodies, other being. Yes,
likely we are one substance, of which mind,

matter, are forms. Voices of past and future speak in ours
and somewhere, all is known—as I know now
father's and son's reality in me.

Poem of the Self

Two birds are perched in the midnight tree.
One whistles, hops, and preens
his golden plumage ceaselessly:
he can't think what he means.

The other—reticent, demure—
watches with golden eyes
till their twinned gaze is merged once more
in the profound sunrise.

The World of Purple Light

In the world of purple light
the people are all plumed in white:
they float and flutter, dart and play,
and plunge into the sapphire spray
of their silent inland seas.

One winter night in '33
I found my way there secretly.
Ancient New York was filled with mist,
its rainy pavements gleaming moist
beneath the street-lamps' yellowing.

At the dark edge of Washington Square
I found the path that leads elsewhere
and followed where it disappears.
Indifferent to the changing years
that path still leads beneath the stones

to an earth estranged—whose sun, subdued,
filters through mists in its colored moods
upon still forests and thick grass
where the white beings turn and pass
in their unhindered solitudes.

They're blissful, but they're self-contained
from never having known our pain,
nor can we guess their lack of love.
Like glad somnambulists they move
as though their stupor were from God.

I looked for a human-seeming face
or one that held at least some trace
of suffering—but there was none
in all that vast communion.
So I returned to my own place.

Then

The freight trains,
        when I was fifteen,
were Satan's bones
shaking in ecstasy—

as the child loves
        what is forbidden
and fears it, too:
that joy of other lives.

Nights of July,
        Connecticut nights,
the summertime earth
sweet in my nostrils,

I thought of girls
        with strange yellow hair,
of dark towns under
the dark night sky

where men watched alone
        in diners, in bars,
under bare lights
in the smell of stations

while trains rumbled out,
        slumbrously tugging,
into deep night . . .
I thought of them waiting—

I, in my bed
        alone, all alone,
not knowing the world
nor where was my home.

The Oppositions

At noon, the furry girls stretch out and talk about fucking
and pat themselves and laugh and touch their fuzzy places.
A wind from the Aegean brings brine against the olives.
Somewhere an eye is watching: from the thyme, perhaps, or the
        jasmine.

Through the leaves a memory glints: of keen Odysseus,
the wanderer who is to come in crafty rectitude—
full of thought, enduring—one who knows his destiny
and in despite of gods makes it his destination.

Can the beast-girls recall the weathered skin of the hero,
or is it some vague foretaste that distends their furry lips,
or yet—in the pure caldron—do they see time's ways all one:
outer and inner being of the great god-and-goddess?

For what are rest and action? Gods in the leaf and blossom,
gods in the sea-spray and storm, oppose us and uphold us,
and all must weave and web: the spider bids us remember
how fatally that wanderer draws the gray-eyed one to his side.

Does it come to the same thing, then—all this strong journeying,
and lassitude of passive bodies in the hot noon sun?
If Odysseus remains, the god is in the fucking;
if he leaves, it is the god within who moves him on.

Etude

There are no peacocks in my house,
the peacocks stride on the lawns;
there are no swans in my strong house,
the lake is clouded with swans.

But dreams of peacocks and of swans
ascend, descend the marble stairs
while moonlight on the terraces
foretells blonde girls in whirling gowns.

A dream of dancers in the snow
(the swans are frozen on the lake)
whirls through the house at 10:00 p.m.
but the clear windows may not break

to fling the dancers out-of-doors
or let the cocks come striding in:
proud cocks would faze the gossamer girls,
their colors rasp my pearly floors.

The swan-necks peck at the slick quick legs
of white girls whisking through the snows.
The strong house glints in the long moonlight—
and dims at dawn in a clamor of crows.

The Reprieve

When the old mirror crashed in the ruined mansion,
released from long imprisonment in time
a red-haired man stepped out into the day.

He saw the littered yard, the clumps of weeds,
a road, a house beyond, a child playing,
and vacant fields strewn with glum debris

that stretched off in the haze to where blunt towers
of a huge somber city rose. Time paused.
The nondescript blinked twice and looked again.

All was quiet, while the child still played.
Far off, a thing flew down the sky, too straight
for any bird. Gone was the mansion, gone

its arms and tapestries, its ambient groves,
and the hidden lake where the chatelaine once bathed—
gone, too, his vaunting dreams of good and evil.

The child cried out, frightened of his beard . . .
Lost in the centuries, the ghost went striding
down that dusty road to find a home.

The Way

The ten thousand things are getting out of hand,
may be headed for the ultimate smashup?

Let them go, let them be,
seeming is not the same as being.

There is a responsibility to the contingent.
Accept it, but remain true to the center,

for the central point is greater than any sphere,
and the Way is there, as it has always been.

Do these two things: you are a sage.
Only begin to do them: you are freed from hysteria,

from the diseased commotion of the age—
free to act cleanly, without regret or apprehension.

Above all, do not use man to help out heaven
or your mind, to help out what you cannot know.

Be yourself, as an old misshapen tree
is itself whether living or dead or beyond life and death.

Then you may move among the myriads
invulnerable, and play your part as well.

Nocturne

Dear Wanderer, on your unimagined journey
I see you pause one night at a scene like this—
a tiny town, four or five houses only,
clustered along the shore of a frozen lake
looked over by the white church from its hill.
It's old New England, it may be Christmas Eve,
the ground is covered white and deep with snow;
outside the inn three carolers are singing
bundled up warm against the frosty night,
but folks are mostly home eating their suppers
while the horses snort and steam in the warm barns.

I see you in white cloak and hood, apart,
standing in snow where you have left no track.
The stars are out, the air is wrenching cold.
With a faint smile you recognize the scene,
rejoicing (you rejoice in all things now),
but have no need to hold it or possess it.
Detached and loving, ready now to leave,
you linger long enough to gaze once more
at two plump children tumbling on the ice.

Song

The devastation
> of being
> proves being
> more fully—
the harp
> of creation
> may reverberate
> more truly
when the great
> final wind
> blows strong
> through its branches
and the soul
> pale and brave
> to its first home
> advances

The Vantage

Death, from where we stand, is nonexistence;
but from another vantage *here* is unreal,
the wrong side of the tapestry—where work is done
that only shows its form on the other side.

Dreams give a sense of this. There is a meaning
that holds us while we're there as part of itself,
but which we lose on the way back. We wake,
feeling deprived of a larger understanding.

Imagine yourself in a huge dark mansion
at night: you're not quite lost, not quite at home,
and free, or so it seems, to move about.
Rooms, halls, stairways—all are still and dark

and yet you know that in that very house
a party is planned and guests are gathering—
talking, laughing, filling the bright-lit rooms—
but you can't find them.   That's the situation.

from

POEMS OF THE TWO WORLDS

(1977)

"At the gate of the worlds stands Truth
and speaks a question into the world."

I

In Silence

Patient things wait in nature,
having undertaken to be only what they are.

Crystals bedded in gneiss,
coral undersea,
robin eggs blue in the nest . . .

"I may love you" (I hear a voice whisper)
"but remain silent—
never come looking.
'You' may have to find me."

"When it rained and rained . . ."

When it rained and rained
and I was a child
I looked from the windows
of "39"
across the slick street and
over the roofs
of three-storey houses—
brick and white trim—
hushed in the wetness
while high in the distance
above dim facades
water towers loomed . . .

until the front door
three flights below
slammed, and my father's voice
rhythmic, searching
rose up the stairwell
calling a name,
the name that was mine—

and I cried out too
naming him back
in our secret tongue
and ran down the deep
stairway to find him:
we met at the heart
of the darkening house

as evening set in . . . Soon
the lights would go on.

Poem of the Gold Coin

A boy in a New York room spellbound by the snow
that drifts down persistently outside the window panes
has closed the door to his room: he moves things about—
games, pencils, books—from desktop to bookcase to floor,
then puts those things back in their places again.
The snow still falls. Nothing in the world has changed.
His desk is painted blue and has twelve cubbyholes
in which are lodged erasers, marbles, and a small
orange-sack filled with worn old Roman coins.
In a corner are stacked frayed piles of pulp magazines.

. . . A boy in Philadelphia watching the rain
that spills down chillingly outside the window panes
runs from his room and up back stairs to the attic
where he opens black rusting trunks and finds old silks,
daguerreotypes, disguises, daggers and
lastly, in the corner of an old brown burlap bag
a single coin—of gold. Spins it in the air!

—All changes then, accelerates—rain, snow,
New York, Philadelphia in alternation
as images of two boys shift, flickering,
and merge at times in a third who is everywhere.

Who is to tell which is real? (If either is.)
Or has each one, perhaps, made up the other?
Or must "I" come to tell it as it were my story?
If so, dark reader, "you" must imagine me.

Another change; and all is still and silent.
Empty fields extend along the shore
on which an empty ocean keeps on breaking . . .
No man nor boy nor beast—at most a bird or two:
space where the mind may seize its vaster being.

The Past

Wind from the frozen lake
in black New Hampshire night
froze the tears to my face.

It was 1936,
deep winter—as I ran
under an aching moon
(quite at the end of my tether)

back to the graceless halls
of that forbidding school
where stunted half-men ruled
our undefended lives.

I spoke to the self within:
"Freeze now and be still—
unyielding as this glass—
then, feel pain no more."

That self obeyed, congealed;
I held it hard within
and thus we two survived.

But I would pay a price
for having a heart turned ice:
years and years must pass
before I loved at last.

Memories

I

A showery summer afternoon: the leaves
dripped softly as I walked down the drenched path
home from a friend's. I liked the touch of rain,

fresh drops shivering down my back as I brushed
through the corner hedge and crossed the lawn to our house.
I ran in, soaking: had the place to myself, I thought.

Up in my room I was naked, drying off
when I saw you standing at the open door—
I ducked down, clutching the towel. "Don't be afraid," you said,

"don't hide from me" (I was crouched down by the bed)
"your parents have gone out. We're alone here now."
You came to me, touched my face. I slowly stood up.

You were Swedish: worked for us as chambermaid.
I remember your eyes, chestnut with amber flaws,
your skin, your mouth—much else besides . . .

Months later, in time of war, you left our house,
married a man with a Slavic name and set up
a home of your own. You came calling once:

buxom, neat, in sleek department-store dress,
your hair in a "permanent wave," you talked to my mother
respectfully commonplace over cups of tea

and when I entered, smiled and shook my hand
and said, "How well you're looking! How is college?"
—while I thought back on that long day of rain

and the fierce freshness of your body's touch.

2

After the opera
night of fog
we went back to your rooms
cooked bacon and eggs

I took off my jacket
you, your long gown
big girl that you were
I was strongly drawn

by rampish plump breasts
held tense in the bra,
I soon set them loose
(you laughing the while)

and licked those large nipples—
we went on from there
to bedroom and bed
there was much to explore

long peaceful billows
of buttock and bust
I was holding a goddess
giantess, beast

in my arms—so it seemed
as you panted and heaved
and when we got going
I was riding huge waves

I was deep in old Egypt
I was fucking a cow!

We yelled and collapsed
flopped down any-old-how
pulled up the mussed covers
and slept until dawn
your slow-breathing body
heavy by mine . . .

When I left, in the chill
of a day just begun,
you reached a big arm out,
said, "Thanks, that was fun."

3
Greenness of spring leaves on
Friday the 13th of
April, where I walked
in Central Park, in coolness.

Sun on my back hinted
its summer fullness
as a light breeze glanced off
the reservoir's face.

A boy in gray sweat-clothes
jogged past sturdily
frayed sneakers splashing
the cinder track—

trucks dumped their dirt at
a black asphalt siding,
a horse-girl cantered by
blonde, straight-backed—

sparrows took their dust-baths
beneath the new-green bushes,
mothers trundled baby-cart
past soiled children playing tag—

as quietly, a primal
fresh smell of water
eased down where my thoughts were clenched
on loves so chancewise lost.

The Door

Stranded late at night when the blackout came
I found I didn't know that city well.
It seemed the streets were all alike:
row after row of blank-faced houses
bulky in the gloom of their high front stoops.

I looked for a main way leading downtown
but kept getting nowhere, or back where I started.
A helmeted warden yelled me to shelter—
soon the bombers would be coming over.

Moon almost full. I paused halfway down
a street like the others with no numbers on the houses
and leaned against a wall in a blotch of darkness.
Somewhere nearby cabbage was cooking,
from an unseen yard a dog yelped twice.

Then—shuffling sounds from close above me
and an old voice gasping, "Rachel! Where are you?"—
gasping and choking, "Oh my God, what have they done to you?"

I chilled inside. Looked up and saw
a dark door opening on emptier darkness
and an old man, stringy-necked, standing and swaying:
he wore a brown robe, his mouth was twisted.

"Is there trouble?" I asked, and went up two steps.
His blurred face blinked, but made no answer.
Across the way a window opened.
"You had best go back in," I said, "there's going to be danger."

"Danger," he moaned—then came words I made no sense of,
and "God God God—the danger's in *there*!"
He turned, pointing, then rushed at the blackness
and vanished, as though he'd been gulped into nothing.
The door closed, all was quiet again.

The bombers didn't come. Alone with the moon
I wandered those empty streets for hours
and when at long last I found the surly warden
there was really nothing at all that could be done.
The houses, the doors were all the same.

1949

1

Under the arbor
      Renée
in your red-and-white-striped shirt
you don't mind
      do you
if I kiss you?

Two or three birds
      in a small flurry
rise to the other world at the tops of the trees—
I like your lips
      (warm, red)
and the hoops that dangle golden from your ears.

2

Come on in, Griselda,
      the water's fine,
black mud bottom
      OK when you get used to it
and no bloodsuckers—
      not in this old pond.

Hovering at the center, I
      can look up at the sky's
pale circle rimmed with tree tops:
      come on in, Gris,
let your big breasts float
      free on the dark water,

I want to see them swaying
      and all that red hair too
in the three o'clockish sun
      as you come
splashing in. We'll
      see the shadows later.

The Letter

He mailed that letter many years ago—
the friend I knew in early army days—
from Germany in 1946.
(He'd stayed on in the service, "marking time.")

It came to my old post after I'd gone,
was forwarded from there to the wrong man
(who strangely had my name) at some remote
specialist-battalion in the mountains,

then—missent once again—crossed the Pacific
and following me where I had never been
moved from one jungle depot to another:
at some it lingered months or even years

before being sent along its stumbling way
at last, with one more wrinkle on its brow.
Old, frayed, and black with changes, it arrived
last night—and brought me good news of myself.

From a Diary

North of 96th where the tracks come out from under
the sun brightens on morning pavements,
the tired air begins to stir.

Puerto Rican streets in Sunday stillness.
An old fat sofa, guts spilling out,
suns itself on the soiled sidewalk.

From a low doorway deep in soot
a child peers, agate-eyed—
a stray dog lopes along, waving his frazzled tail.

The breeze blows grit into my eyes
as I pass a vacant lot girt with rotting fence-boards.
Stevenson's face looks out from tattered posters
alert and fatigued, somehow beyond it all.
"We must look forward to great tomorrows."

Over on Lexington the bars are closed,
the pawnshops gated tight—but the corner luncheonette,
where you can get the greasiest fried eggs in town,
is doing good business with its counters jammed.

A skinny girl passing by gives me the eye,
I smile and look down. A newspaper blows past.

Down the street a nun—thin, white-faced—
gathers her children about her: but now they're on top of me
in a scraggly column, running and shoving their way
toward the parish school of St. Francis de Sales.
The nun's face is lined, mouth down-drawn, but from the eyes
something fragile glints that may be happiness . . .

Or so I propose—as I wonder why it all
happens the way it happens, and what will befall
myself and the world, as time runs out—

and tell myself at last to be still and not mind.
Today, held firm, is my tomorrow.

—New York, 1953

Exotica

1
White gown transparent on her,
"torse and limb shone through"
        (in winter, in New York, in '42)—
outside, a few lights in the dark apartments.

2
Her body by candlelight had that elegant look—
        but eyes were bruised and "tragic"
the house half-shrouded for a winter of war,
the letter—shriveled like a stricken moth . . .

3
Bought girl, braceleted Arab, Zayn-al-Mawasif,
dance! as prelude to the hungry night.

4
Her spirit moved towards me across the harbor,
over the water it moved like a shadow of light.

Spirit is tenuous. *She* was far away.
The air moved damply to the foghorn's groaning.

5
Too late . . .
rain . . .
That bitch Mathilde takes on another man . . .

6
Who used to read to me of Eloisa's love
in the park, late afternoons, by lake of swans . . .
who with white weak hands,
turning the pages in a whiter sadness?

7
Touch me not with gauzy hair
                or skimmering nipple,
ephemerid!

8
Steeped in the cunt
my deep descent—
freedom beyond what's human.

9
Russet-brown, copper-pink
bold-blotched with black and sinewy—
mute spirit of the brushlands,
Surucucu the quick-striking.

10
Anteaters
in dreams
were a horror to Alexandra . . .

11
Misunderstanding on the plane to Cairo!
Carlotta went to sulk behind the Sphinx
                while I—immaculate, estranged—
turned my thoughts to the endless plains of Kenya.

12
Lizard in the sunshine,
lemur under the moon,
she fled the city of
my ten thousand faces.

13
Paris. The hotel. The morning after.
I felt remote from the sound of Tanya's laughter.

Wanted to get at the news in the morning papers—
more or less indifferent to last night's capers.

14
Blue-lashed
in the smoky moon,
Aissa . . .
             (phony Arab name!)
jazzing me for francs near the docks at Cherbourg.

15
La Malbaie: in the herb-garden by twilight
at summer's end I caught the "swift Camilla":
we rode each other through the purple night.

16
Never forget. The cool and gritty wind
over the New York streets those early winter
mornings of the 1930s, when
I looked out from my window all alone . . .

II

From a Forgotten Book

When we stormed the city Sirk in the mountains
we put to the sword that foul, misshapen people:
cut down men, women, children where they stood.
Their corpses choked the streets, dogs drank their blood.

Four hundred of us slaughtered forty thousand
joyously, for we did not like their smell.
We gave ourselves to war as to a goddess;
each time we struck we struck to kill.

Spirits of our fathers woke in us
dooming to hell that stinking maggot-swarm
of soft manipulators, puny cheats
who held the honor of the brave in scorn.

I found my destined one: small, sly and fat,
leaving behind a spoor of squirrel slime
he turned, hyena-faced, to bare his teeth
and giggle, as I struck him the last time.

Our fathers know us. Violent and true
followers of the ultimate great Khan
foredoomed to dwindle down the stony years,
we've eaten death but never tasted fear.

I took my red-haired sister to my bed
that night, for each had killed a hundred men,
and felt her savage body leap with mine.
Then like two wolves replenished in their den

austere in furs beneath our snowy tent
we sucked the mountain air chill under stars—
our minds appeased, our bodies deeply spent,
while absence glittered in our perfect hearts.

Centaurs

Centaurs' habits are not of the nicest.
At parties they'll get drunk and start to fight
and smash the furniture—what's more, they're certain
to put their hands on every woman in sight.

They sprout such huge erections it's unnerving
(their throbbing members swell to sapling size)—
then as if proud of these uncouth protrusions,
rearing, they'll challenge you to feast your eyes.

Once in this state, of course, they'll stick it into
woman, mare, cow—whatever has a cunt—
release the enormous flood, then pull out crudely
and canter off with no more than a grunt.

They stuff themselves at table, belch and guzzle,
shouting "More food!" when others try to talk;
right in plain view they'll raise their tails up idly,
dropping their dung where others wish to walk.

Yet—they're acknowledged wise, and the old medals
portray them noble-browed, stern-faced, serene
with full combed bears and philosophic features.
Was there a balance struck? If so, what does it mean?

We've learned of double natures and their conflicts
(the "lower" burns, the "higher" seeks control),
perhaps should look on them as localizations,
chancewise revealed, of an unbounded whole

that's humorous, irrational, impassive,
yielding no "clear ideas" to any "mind,"
graspable only as night-skies are grasped
in hopeless reach of love by those born blind:

for cold-cast eye may not deny the sorrow
of the great surging brute below, whose lust
must find fulfillment in its each occasion
as body comes to know itself in dust.

Bianca

Where are you, Bianca Capello, beautiful child
whose "deadly hand has faln upon your lord"?
I knew you in my youth's ambitious years—
now in my strength I summon you again.

You overreached . . . It's purgatory, perhaps,
this being born again life after life—
in the same form or almost, with the same eyes
reflecting a deep underworld of meaning,

yes, all this beauty, all this grace renewed—
subject to fat-faced husband, yelping brats
who spoil as they grow and break your heart at last.
—If so, there is an end . . . I saw you once

behind a Tuscan albergo, looking down
a scuffed slope where your five pups were howling
egged on by the idiot-grinning father. God!
You had an inward look. Were you thinking of poison?

So stern your face, severe. Wind lifted your hair.
Should I have said "I love you" in Italian?
I didn't: something there not to be touched
but left in peace for long unravelings.

Just a few words then, dear, to mark your doom:
She was born near Venice and she used to love
those trees that mutter to the western sky
at evening. The rest is still to come.

Mary

As soon as Jesus was dead and buried, the rumors
began to spread of various manifestations:
a page was turned, a new strange chapter begun.
Mary, however, spent most of her time at home

quietly living her life out. Certain things
remembered or discovered, which she had fixed
long ago in her heart, commanded her still.
Her life only was hers, after all. She knew it.

And so, when important persons came to call
asking her questions about her son—Who was he?
What had he claimed to be?—she only smiled
and gave no answer. They went off displeased,

but she knew very well there were no words
for her to utter. She could only be—
as pledge of truth that dwells beneath all words
and lives on darkly flowing, like a stream.

The years passed. She was more and more herself:
gentler, sterner to the end. No need
to call that fragile body up to heaven
who knew her heaven within, and died content.

Hideyoshi

After the last battle,
the enemy having been cut to pieces,
he rode a short distance from the field
and dismounted.

Sat in his armor on the grass
and gave word to his staff
that he wished to make a flower-arrangement—
they, however, lacked the equipment.

So he took a bucket, and his horse's bit
(which he hung by one ring from the bucket-handle)
and rigged them into a flower-holder,

then with his bloody sword
cut wild blossoms and grasses
and in an hour's silence
composed a subtle and delicate combination . . .

Those whom he had conquered
he now must judge:
he wished a mind clean-purged
of violence and ardor.

Pirate Poem

Behind the mountain's belly-button
(press it and it lets you in)
pirates hid ten chests of gold
guarded by a skeleton.

In one scanty hand he held
a sword upraised to strike you down;
the other clutched a blanching skull
the mirror-likeness of his own.

Above, on the fresh mountainside
where austral breezes stirred sparse shrubs,
couched in a higher, cooler cave
a she-bear nursed her huddled cubs.

The pirates went their several ways:
some were hanged and some were drowned
and some retired as country men,
but one returned to that far ground

twenty years later, found the navel,
pressed it—and it let him in—
stepped across the threshold, saw
by torch's light the skeleton,

which gently set down skull and sword,
stood up, stretched out imploring hands . . .
The other turned and fled. And fell—
and bleached white on the island sands.

The Rescue

Around the old old islands
      old old crocodiles swim
eye sockets like croquet wickets
      glinting in the sun.

Their wicked eyes transfix you,
      little naked man
splashing from the sea-wreck
      of the great ship *Caliban*

to those green Encantadas—
      at least, that's your idea,
despite the tricky creatures
      grinning from ear to ear.

You head for the far bull's-eye
      through circles of bright teeth—
there, at last you've made it,
      hard land beneath your feet.

You stumble through the shallows
      retching up bile and brine,
crawl across crusted ledges
      aglitter with sea-shine

and now, passing the tide-mark,
      shed weak and thankful tears . . .
Something's a little wrong, though,
      there's not much greenness here—

just black volcanic scourings
      to scorch the tender skin
and sun and rock and tortoises
      and sea-birds shrieking down

the winds that blow from elsewhere.
 Is "elsewhere" home? You've come
where there's no getting back without
 another, longer swim.

The Exiles

At night they moved from room to room glinting,
with under the nightdress a bangle or two
and wine at the bedside in tall decanters
in which to pledge the perilous name.

They felt they were doomed most likely, but tried
each day to deny the future, the past,
as they rode brown fields on horseback
revisiting the further farms.

Deep autumn: tinge
of apples dusky on the air
when nights drop sharply down, and dawns
reveal quick scatterings of frost.

Letters arrived from time to time
mostly with word of deaths:
the ways of the fathers and mothers were strange
but not as strange as the chill present.

How would it end—this game, this dream—
in sudden silence all about
with black skies falling to the earth,
or by slow sequence of cessations?

The world in sum was muck, they thought,
paltry and diseased—
and if indeed a god held sway
he should have worked first on himself,

done something for his private lacks
before presuming to bring forth
other minds touched with his malaise
and dim resentment of the void.

They saw their shadows, caught in his huge mirror.

Autobiographies

for Charles K. Warner

I

I lay on my back in Portugal
the storks were flying over
    white green white
on their way from the Coto Doñana
    white white blue
numina enskied:

I watched them through the fingers of one hand.

2

I am up at five, have coffee, read my paper on the terrace—
at eight, close shutters and blinds: the rooms are sealed.
In a morning twilight (one window alone half open)
I do some writing at the cardinal's desk
then go out, take care of my errands and pay a few calls.
I like to get my work done before noon—

Have lunch at one, make love, and sleep till four
while down in the piazza the workmen are asleep
lying, their heads on their arms, full length on the pavement
and the little boys curl up in the shade of the columns.
The city sounds are muted; the air is still.
This is the quietest time.
                   Soon after four
the seabreeze comes in and life begins again.
Tea on the terrace: the streets are filled with people.
The girls, always so charming, are wearing pink muslin this year
and dinner seems to be pushed back later and later.
We seldom dine alone. It's a time for friends,
for candlelight—
cold chicken, a light white wine, fresh fruit and ices . . .

At night we sit out in the coolness, under stars.

3

I found the place at last—
twenty-five miles due west
of the humid capital:
an inconspicuous cluster of huts
in a small jungle clearing.
A brown man in fatigues
was patrolling, carbine ready.
Insects hummed.
I climbed into the branches
of a low tree, and waited.

Just after dark a storm broke—
solid rain like a lake overturned
flare after flare of sheet lightning—
I hunched, shifted my grip
and heard soon, under the thunder,
a dull groaning and clanking.
Trucks creeping down the rutted path
broke into the clearing—four of them.
They stopped, men jumped down,
others ran out from the huts
and after some shouting in Spanish
began the unloading.
I could see, by the intermittent glare,
the long thin crates that held the guns.

Two nights later at the waterfront bar
the strip-teaser, to finish off her act,
thrashing naked on her back on the narrow stage
spread her thighs screaming and inserted a banana—
to the huge approval of the military.

4
Arrived at the foot of the Maiden:
glaciers, torrents
nine hundred feet in visible descent
and minute by minute avalanches falling
like thunder.

        I gathered snow there,
crushed it to hardness in my hands
while sound of cowbells
rose from the remote pastures.
Saw no man. The air, distilled,
was sharper than on a January day at home.

And then the storm came on—
hail, thunder, lightning, all in their perfection
beautiful as the last day of the Eon,
the day of finished things.
I thought of other lives
predestined as my own—
fine-textured, diverse, each imbued with its own finality.
Looked upward through the hail:
the torrent's shape was curved over the rock
not mist nor water but something in between,
tail of a white horse streaming in the wind.

5
A narrow room with rush blinds
straw carpet
a table and mat—
the mind being calm and at ease
simple beauties gratify the eye
—as, behind the house, a grassy slope that goes down to the river—
and common daily sounds delight the ear.

To hold to the simple present.
A meal of vegetables,
soup of boiled greens, will do:
the mind, cleared of sediment,

resting on its emptiness
mastering the great principle—
shoes of coarse hemp
robes of coarse cloth
granting body such ease as it requires
until its day of death.

III

Two Poems to a Dead Woman

1

Lady, the strange malignancy
which you called "love": in two more years
or three, it would have finished me.

You sought chiefly my misery
and pain, took pleasure in my tears.
Lady, you were malignancy

itself, playing your games with me,
tormenting me with guilt and fear,
twisting the love I had in me

to my own shame and injury
until I hated my young years.
This was your strange malignancy—

loathing yourself, you hated me
who would have freed you from your fears
could I have forced myself to be

the doom you sought so stubbornly!
—But I was rescued by the years
from that perverse malignancy:

they finished you, and set me free.

2

The whitish dawn had just appeared
with "rose and gold crowning her head"
when my dark soul, returned from dream,
slid through the window to my bed.
I woke. My soul seemed not my own
so mixed it was with every form
of man and woman I have known:
it lingered in that shapeless swarm.

And then I saw your shade that stood
naked and hateful in the gloom,
a beast from sleep's foul underwood
astir in the uncertain room:
the stabbing serpent-breasts outthrust,
the weasel-glitter in the eyes,
the belly-fold and wicked tuft
of jungle-black between the thighs.

What need I more of death (I thought)
who used to hold this fatal thing,
this corpse, in love's embrace? But then
the soul itself began to sing
a cool refrain of chiming verbs
austere upon the rising day—
and you, poor brute, spat out once more
your futile curse, and fled away.

Grandfather Poem

Grandfather stepped out from the clock
at 2:00 a.m. one summer night.
He had been dead for forty years.
He gave his grandchildren a fright.

They asked him why he had come back.
"I haven't been far off," he said.
"I never liked you much, alive,
  but things are cooler now I'm dead,

  greener, deeper, firmer-set
  in a dimension that gives ease—
why not reach back with part of me
into time's old complexities?

For something of the all I am
was formed here, when all's said and done,
though now I walk a wider range
and scarce recall the game I won."

Enigmas

Aubade
Who has hold of Juliet's nipples
ramming her from behind?
Is it her very own Romeo,
or the sardonic weathered friend—
even perhaps her doddering sire
incestuously inclined?

It doesn't matter to the cat
creeping at dawn along the tiles
back to his interior self:
no thought may ambush that sly track.

The scowling cousin skulks in outer shadow.
The pumping mounts up to a brace of screams.
Old nurse in her bed turns snorting, sighing—
eases herself into commodious dreams.

Thaw
Shape a couple out of mist
or shall it be a delicate hound
snowy-pale in January?

Don't expect to hunt till dawn
if no dawn is entertained
by those who are its denizens.

So dance with me, Miss Talleyrand,
in the broken-down chateau—
red berries gleam out from those vines!

In thaws of yet another March
the ice breaks, releasing death
which until now has seemed a mirror.

Shame
"I am two days from death
and I have no name."
What shall I call you then?
"Call me shame,
bonerack, stench, and living corpse
with a hey and a ho and back to the dust."

Ugly shame,
stupid shame,
old shame two days from death!
Grin if you can
while I sing you a song
of what poor shame is worth.

Mirror
The mirror turns black.
The night walks in from the sea.
There are no more faces
to watch the heron's slow flight along the shore.

Dark sand is mixed
with moistly shining stones
along the levels your naked feet once knew,

while other mirrors under sea
retain your shape implicitly
and the winds racket through the huge house and return to their
        island.

No faces any more.
Only—empty places
dark-tinctured by the sea,
awaiting those in the mirror who won't come back.

The Closed House

It remained silent
            two or three centuries
windows closed,
white shutters hooked from the inside.

Outside the birds changed
            their customs, their plumage.
Certain cities dared approach—
then, withdrawing, crumbled.

Thin bands of sungleam
            flittered in those rooms.
No doubt they were the secret,
no doubt they remained

after the house sank
            one bright winter morning
down through black subsoil
under gritty tree-roots . . .

Moles delved about it,
            worms paid their visits,
still the house persisted
intact and serene

almost as though retaining
            a larger life's reflections
that moved once through those open doors
and would at leisure be resumed.

Bones

The bones go under the soil, under the soil
at year's end the bones go under the soil—
sometimes they wave red flags
sometimes they speak not at all

The bones are boats that go sailing in the black ground
clean through the earth and out the other side
in an everyday kind of way
into the sun again

The bones speak to the birds, the birds sing back
but the language is lost before it comes to the ears
of fools who run to and fro
between the birds and the bones

I killed a fool once and drank blood from his skull
and taking his bony fingers in my hand
asked him where he expected to go:
he didn't say yes, he didn't say no

Bones have a home underground or so I'm told.
They are themselves the city in which they dwell
and have a meaning, too, since they once were we:
another meaning is coming, wait and see

Maitreya

Life is a flame (he said)
before the wind blows . . .

life is a flame
as though in itself enduring.

Not much to be done, when all is said,
about that wind.

After a breath or two—
or a billion years it may be—

speech to be extinguished,
the mobile body shudder to its end

and the words array themselves
on a high meadow, burning.

IV

Poems of the Two Worlds

I

The beginning is a cold wind
or the taste of mineral beneath the grass

or being lifted above the winter city
demonic in dusky air

as, to the midward of my journey,
in a February of frigid moon

the sordid clock tower on East Ninety-Fourth
shone—and in Maine on the frozen point

while waves broke perishing across the rocks
breathing the icy night my heart near stopped:

and if it had, it had been as well
in the long gaze from the second world

these our deep pains are no matter—
in the night wind the stopped heart rises

rises and sings on its recovered journey
following the dark-winged intermediary

escorted by his hawks and owls:
the beginning is the cold breath

of stone and crystal at the roots—
a whisper of water from the night side—

the second world where the dead walk arm in arm,
perfected ones garbed in their destinies,

breathing their power into these airs
through the vague intervals of matter

where the circling desolate heart
awaits in turn its liberation.

2
From the Crab's whirl
                from beyond the stars
                            from blackness
a hand thrusts,
        shakes pepper from a pot:
the seeds sift through the universe in clouds,
each speck bears in itself Homunculus
crouched and scowling, thinking human thoughts . . .

The golden Egg is opening,
                        the pepper seasons it
with chance
                with abnormality of change
                            with life
that happens as it happens in its drift
as God is happening unto himself.

It all unfolds, by chance, just as it had to—
just as it must, though no one made it happen:
it comes
        departs
                    is a retaining Mind
and Not-mind, and what exceeds those both.

After breakfast, God takes his random walk
in the cool glades where nothingness has being:
his thoughts rejoin themselves beneath the trees.

3

The dark one crouching in his cave alone
withdraws strange emeralds from the sulphur spring.
The feckless gulls are morselling the ledge
above a nameless ocean's million blades.

A single sail on all that blue: it's Cook,
Bougainville or St. Brendan, or maybe
Madoc the bastard or the long-lost sire,
homing at last, of Victoria Rapahango.

Brilliant voyagers of the mind's clear stream,
sharp-featured entities with eyes of gold,
they emanate from the great throning Dream
that lurks behind this jettison of sky.

The mind dilates; contracts again, absorbs
its jewels in a deathly inner space
where yet some quick chance touch may magically
open granite doors to those bragging waves

that haunt the dark one in his reverie
with images of fate and what's beyond—
even as the gulls fly whitely forth and back
across the real and the unreal ocean . . .

The voyager still lives within the legend,
the utterer still mutely shapes the tale;
when the dark eye spies out the lonely sail
then seafarer and cave-dweller are one

upon the bright, illimitable sphere
where shapes of life emergent from deep dream
wax, wane and blend themselves within the Change—
until the dreamer lift his changeless eye.

4
Komë Berenikes floating
		in the sea with jellyfish . . .
Rinsings of dismembered wrecks
		glimmer outside Gulnar's halls
as the drowned wights light their lamps
		phosphorescent on the rocks
where her whiskered doublemen
		display their swaying testicles.

Changelings keep the stars in mind
		each to sink his secret being
deep through the reflective dark
		where urchins vibrate in the mud
and the secular Crab awaits
		minglings of a second sun.

Stars who know their living names
		coolly urge that long awareness.
Forms within the crystal dusk
		whirl and coalesce in bliss
and lots are drawn! The worlds are one.
		Twins come now unto their own.

. . . Silent in great space the seal
		swims between the stars.

5
Pêcheur, pêcheur, avez-vous vu
la reine des ombres, la blanche Dahut?
Revisiting the Breton shore
on coal-black horse, long hair blown back,
hard on the heels of her shadow pack
she hunts the weakling dead once more.

In feeble panic see them fly,
misshapen dim nonentities
aquiver with the self's disease,
who live their lives within a lie.
The hounds' white teeth shall rend their flesh,
each coward fragment feel her lash!

Enough of that. The meaning seen
a quarter-century ago
when the dark Self put on her show
perhaps conceals what she would mean.
Let's think so, friends! whose living heads
I saw driven down among those dead.

It would appear that you are damned,
but I'll not be the one to say it.
If there's a debt, and you must pay it,
pay it you shall at her command—
proud living Bitch of my desire
from whose deep eyes my eyes take fire—

no, Heaven's not always for the meek!
But a secret's here I may not speak . . .
Past the still fisher by the stream
I thread my way through tangled paths
backwards from the place of wrath
to shallows of a nearer dream.

6

A rose dawn, in smoke, over the East River:
light is reflected from the keel of clouds
along Park Avenue's soiled streaks of snow.
My sense attends the shiftings of the cold.

Something—something reaches out behind the semblance:
dimness with claws, brutal and serene.
The sun rises across pale roofs of asphalt.
A car stops at the red on ninety-fifth, which clicks to green.

A man with a briefcase hurries to the corner,
hails a cab, speeds off in a spray of slush;
the newspaper boy in scarlet stocking cap
trundles his squeaking cart from block to block . . .

How shall I fix your shape or speak your name,
great glow-eyed Cat crouched at the roots of being?
This traffic of shadows between dark and light
obscures the pure insistence of your gaze.

And yet, foreshortened, as from invisible sunlight,
it's in that exacting gaze the shadows live—
rehearse the permutations of their fates
and win such vision as may view themselves.

Somewhere, in an antiworld,
a man has risen and looks out from his window;
his face is mine, but if we should shake hands
all worlds, thoughts, gods would find their fiery end,

being reduced to your simplicity,
God, who are Any, All, and None—in one.
Now, please, retire; and claws be sheathed.
Cold and bright the day's begun.

V

Saying

There is always another way to say it.

As when you come to a dusty hill and say,
"*This* is not the hill I meant to climb.
That one I've perhaps climbed already—see,
there it looms, behind me, green with trees."
And then climb as you can the present hill.

Or when you walk through a great childhood forest
latticed with sun, carpeted in brown pine,
knowing the one you were and the one you are,
and think, "I shall not speak this forest's name
but let it densely live in what I am . . ."

The saying changes what you have to say
so that it all must be begun again
in newer reconcilings of the heart.

Blue Hill Poems

1

The green men march along the ground
into the thickets without sound
then swarming forth, they march once more
where the cool grasses edge the shore.

Half-stillness . . . and translucent mutter—
light skirmishings of wind and water—
in glimmering thousands at midday
blue Christs are striding on the bay.

2

We have acquaintances
                    up at the quarry:
a lettuce-green frog balances in the shaded corner
nose and eyes peering up from the shallows,
a water-boatman with scarlet head
glides along the watertop (he doesn't like my feet),
dragonflies in tandem hover and glisten,
a chipping sparrow rustles in the low laurel-bush
—there he goes with his *click click click*
as in the great midst we swim alone,
                    naked and serene.

3

Eyes looked at me from the old stone wall
down among roots at the bay's edge.
I said, "Eyes—believe I am not here at all
but only a spirit passes by
and you can't see spirits or know what they are
beyond these quiverings of salty air
as you reach from your lurking-place of leaves and pebbles
across the granite ledge."

Time and place made no reply.
The eyes awaited no command.
There was nothing, perhaps, to understand
in all that glowing sun-drenched sky
and wave-sheet mirroring in to land.

Eyes looked on eyes, being self-imbued,
then those eyes faded and mine turning away
to distant borders of the resplendent day
released themselves from the doubled view,
fixing now in diminished gaze
(as though that gaze alone held good)
the circle of a single world
bedazzling in its solitude.

And wave, and boat, and bird were silent
crystallizations of a mind
seeking the union known by sense
when senses give back from their strivings
into the brightness that is blind.

Eyes then denote a center of being
with radius of sense and comprehension
and what the being is, the eyes don't know,
unapt to turn back on themselves
or look behind. Being is known only
by being itself, in its own dimension—
yes, eyes are holes in the world's face, through which something
    else
does its own huge seeing.

4
The worm beneath the grass
tingles against moist roots,
the yellow jacket drills
deep into pulpy fruit:

a day of rippling airs
and golden undertones—
barefoot we wander down the beach
culling its whitest stones.

5

(North Sedgwick)

In the deep afternoon
        August shade
at the edge of shimmering
        asphalt, three
Indian children are sitting.

Micmacs from Canada
        down for the
blueberries, they have brilliant
        muskrat eyes,
inquiring feminine faces.

In a moment we have
        driven past,
retaining though the imprint:
        T-shirts' pale
lavender, deep blue dungarees.

6

Do not wait for the owl to come out
before you start your games!

The owl sleeps in the tree all day,
at night he comes out to hunt and hoot.

He sleeps in the old weary pine-tree
but at night his eyes are whirlpools

and when he flies over the house his shadow
carries the house with it above the pines

to a shining lonely place where calm eyes watch
in the moonlight—but our eyes are always closed.

7
Nothing is better than seaweed on rocks
and barnacles that scrape
and the harsh rub of granite
and the wind from the south bringing salt

except the sight of you naked—
Venus of every day—
arms lifted, balancing lightly
as you enter the naked wave.

8
At the tide pool pocketed in broken granite
lives converge.
A gull skims over; flies hum
and circle, settle on the scummed salt surface.
I lie on the rocks as flat as I am able
eyes focused on the smaller world
as a bee gleams by, lazingly.
Beneath, in sedimented green
a white-purple starfish curls,
his inner tendrils moving delicately,
and a crab size of my thumb
pale-green as a young apple
scuttles under green-brown seaweed
with a clean movement of legs.

The sun bakes my back,
granite edges dint my thighs—

I raise my head. Out and beyond
the silly sailboats skimmer on the bay
(summer sailors at their Saturday races)
and the sun is high and gold and somewhere else,
somewhere where life is rare—
it's as though, in the deep day's expanded gaze,
you were extracted from the immediate
into a realization beyond what you knew.

Who speaks to me of the Person in the sun—
in annihilation's blaze the one who sings?

Here, though, at my center of things
where the heat is intimate, intense
I'm pressed down hard into my own self-knowledge
and the world of private understandings:
no vision but one's own
as rock and weed endure
and the stubborn crab maintains a brief existence
becoming a part of self and self's perception
(time drawing still and holding
steady in this clear light).
"What is small survives," I speak the words
remembering how it all in time will end—
"what is small prevails."
I whisper it to the sun and to myself.

9
Cricket in the kitchen,
        you hum a pleasing tune
as I fix myself a pineapple and rum:

I may not wish to see you
        but I like your self-assertion.
To your health, then—little bird of the end of summer!

10

Oh, unapproachable One,
whom yet through this night of soft rain
I feel coolly stir at my heart,
through all my deaths and my lives
may I flow in your presence, and sing—
as I follow the shapes of my selves—
your glory, your peace, your abundance.

11

October in Maine. The human touch:
outboards, power saws, and guns.
A landscape fading into death endures
the idiot stutterings, fatalistically.

I listen and I think. Where might be
a true New England emptied of the human?
Forest, lake unswerving through their changes
old as the ultimate earth, fresh as this dawn
and unwatched always but by one still man—
or man and woman, waiting quietly.

Whale Poem

All of the bones of five toes are in each of his paddles
and under the blubber the bones of unused hind legs.

The tail (unlike a fish's, horizontal)
is rudder and propeller both, and drives him
with strength of seventy horses abruptly down
hundreds of feet to depths at which his body
must bear many tons of pressure per square inch.

Rising, he may release the used-up breath
just before reaching the surface: at such times
a mixture of water and breath blows up from the sea.

I read about him first in Kipling's story—how
the sailor he swallowed foxed him by blocking his throat—
but the truth about the baleen whale was more surprising.
His mouth is a maze. He has no teeth.
Enormous plates of horn in the upper jaw,
frayed at the edges as though rough-combed for use,
lie flat, toward the throat, when the mouth is closed—
when it opens, they are raised and hang down like fringed curtains.
As he swims through the sea open-mouthed, a living cavern,
thousands of little life forms are trapped in the fringes;
when the mouth closes, the water strains out at the sides
but these remain and fall down on the tongue to be swallowed.
(They have to be small—his throat couldn't take in a herring!)

A sperm whale, on the other hand, can swallow a Jonah
or something still larger. His mouth takes up one third
the length of a body that may extend sixty feet.
The sperm oil lies in a cavity alongside his head
and ambergris—used as fixative in making perfumes—
may, when he's in poor health, form in his guts.
It used to be found in great masses, floating on southern seas . . .

The whale I saw in '49 or '50
was a smaller kind, maybe a grampus—I'd say
about twenty-five feet. He surfaced off our boat
(Eddie Sherman's lobster-boat, which Dr. Moorhead
had chartered for his annual fishing trip:
we had our lines out, anchored in the mouth of Blue Hill Bay)
one hundred yards out to sea, and blew and spouted—
a hollow whistling more vibration than sound—
then sank, and surfaced once more about ten minutes later
on our other side, a little bit closer—and we laughed.
We got the message: greatness, freedom, and ease.

They're mammals; the mothers nurse their young.
We hunt them, sink our barbs into their flesh—
using explosives now in harpoons—
hoist the vast bleeding bodies to the decks
of "factory ships," where the live flesh is rent from the bone.
They may have thoughts in their heads: we do not know.

Sometimes I think of the great sum of pain
endured by inoffensive giant bodies
torn, ripped, chopped, dismembered in their millions
by the sharp tricks of a smart race of maggots.
Is there justice in the universe? We'd better hope not.

I had a dream once, in which I was swallowed by a whale
and thought it was the end and something horrible—
but it all opened up, like the Mammoth Cave,
in long strange hallways—stalactites, stalagmites gleaming—
and light in the distance where someone was waiting for me.

They may have thoughts—we do not know. But far
beneath the surface, where a few still live and play,
they summon each other in high-pitched signalings
and sing deep day-long songs we'll never learn.

"Anger at my heart one April morning..."

Anger at my heart one April morning
and by St. Vincent Ferrer's the magnolias in bloom . . .

You wrestle with yourself as with an angel
who leaves you maimed and scarred. Let him prevail,
he'll weigh you down into nonentity,
but if you win, it's only for the day:
he's always back to try you out again.

I saw my fellow once, up in the sky
riding a cloud above the Chrysler Building
whose spire gleamed in gold—but what his face looks like
I haven't known, for always in our struggles
he keeps his head turned downward and away.

At the circus a few days ago a clown
fell from a high wire into the lions' cage
which—for publicity—served as a net.
The creatures roared, showed anger, but the tamer
held them at bay while the hurt clown rolled free.
He's in the hospital now, recovering;
soon will be fit to do his act again.

Admirable, to define yourself this way?
Yes, partly, for the courage and persistence.
But what's the final sense, if you know you yearn
to be at one with the prime animal
who'd clasp you to him in his raging love—
the six-winged beast all circleted with eyes?

You try to talk to God, to come to terms.
Not easy—particularly if that self
you see as you, is grasped too definitely.
Too easy then to start the act all over,
God fading into a sort of wishfulness—
but let that sense of self blur a bit, grow vague,

you'll slip through these big temporary meshes
and find yourself. Where? In the world where all is known.
For suddenly the wrestlers disengage,
each seeing the angel in the other's eye—
the angel who, in each, is the same "I"—
and all is stilled within the sun's great blaze.

The passions then, released, ride the high winds
and God himself roars with them and rejoices.

Being, I

God
sitting at midday outside the cafe at Aix
where it had brightened after quick-scattering showers,
sitting with a half-empty glass just taking his time
(you didn't see him come, won't notice when he leaves)

or on a fine spring afternoon in New York
stepping out upon a never-used balcony
overlooking Madison, enjoying the hot sun
and the stink of traffic, biding there a while
before turning back inside where no one will know

or watching the olive girls play tag at evening
in Rio, in the Jardim Botanico
pausing in the long aisle of elegant palms
to enjoy the dancing breasts and gleaming eyes
while high in the dusk one star begins its gleaming—

he always seems to be making the best of things,
pleasantly unconcerned . . . but you're never sure
what is his real being, what his "mere appearance"
or whether it matters. How can you tell, after all,
since he may be "infinity" or just a wisp of cloud?

The realization is somehow in *you*. Because, of course,
there's no meaning in his great Name: it's all in the glimpse.

Being, II

God always was
but never knew his meaning
until he had creation
to see in, as a mirror.

Felt the stain of suffering
as share of the world's being—
then, a shock of freedom
opening to his joy.

For one swerve of sameness
was stranger to himself there
coming to new seeing
as of a hunger sphere

that was his own dear body
pure, impure together,
juncture of his dreams,
and sacred wastes beyond.

"In a five-minute stillness in September . . ."

In a five-minute stillness in September
the sunlight not yet departing from the goldenrod
that straggled down to shore's edge

it seemed all at once as if all might be understood—
if not articulately, at least in depth of heart—
by some less privileged life form,

some being that would move, eat, procreate, and so on
but without the cutting edge of arrogance
that so disfigures our kind,

whose brain, pale instrument too fine for its data,
will, left with nothing better to do,
multiply small distinctions

endlessly, uselessly in a tight compulsion
to impose its structure on the stuff of existence—
which indeed will bend itself

but only up to a certain unassayable point
beyond which, if the mind wander, it wanders untethered
from the glad solemn animal

cleaving to the heart of time, and holding in its own heart
as fulfillment of joy and pain (on days of September sun)
the certitude of being.

Music

from the Han Fei Tzu

In ancient times
the Yellow Emperor
assembled the spirits at the summit of Mount T'ai.
It was in autumn, when the dying begins.

Tigers and wolves in his vanguard
ghosts and elementals roaming behind
he rode in an ivory carriage, drawn
by six slouched dragons.
Overhead, through the chill sky, phoenixes soared.

The Wind Lord cleared his passage
the Rain Master sprinkled his road
and a god kept pace with the linchpin,
a god whose name was unknown.

Standing, then, at the cold peak
amid thin swirls of cloud
he called the beings together
from all the realms and quarters

and with them, created music:
those austere intervals of the *chüeh* mode,
the saddest and the purest.

Winter Poem

We made love on a winter afternoon
and when we woke, hours had turned and changed,
the moon was shining, and the earth was new.
The city, with its lines and squares, was gone:
our room had placed itself on a small hill
surrounded by dark woods frosted in snow
and meadows where the flawless drifts lay deep.
No men there—some small animals all fur
stared gently at us with soft-shining eyes
as we stared back through the chill frosty panes.
Absolute cold gave us our warmth that night,
we held hands in the pure throes of delight,
the air we breathed was washed clean by the snow.

First of May

Through slats of our half-open shutters
I see green branches stirring
of lindens in hot sun
in the courtyard of St. Sergius's across the street.

Here in the blue studio
that strong light is subdued
as it angles in through the slats and across the bookshelves.
I have opened one window
and sit here in my usual chair
while sounds of spring come freely in from the street:
the screams of children playing ball
clop of ball on pavement
calls, complaints of mothers
squeak of delivery-bikes
bellowing of the old concierge at the Rumanian Embassy
who directs the parking of cars—
behind it all, the hustle of traffic going up and down Park.

Our indoor colors are rich in the afternoon glow.
On the chest your red-framed Picasso poster lies
waiting until we find the right precise spot for it.
Over the mantel Duke William's tapestry hangs tawny-bright.

I am thinking of a poem.
I am thinking also of making love to you
on our Portuguese bed, the moment you arrive.
Meanwhile, someone downstairs has begun cooking supper early
and even as I write, the light grows subtly cooler.

—It was not long ago—two weeks or a little more—
that on a chilly midnight
we awaited on this street
the procession to the Tomb:
those ancient bearded priests, those crucifers icons and banners

rounding the corner of the house built by the Chairman of the New
    York Central
passing through the court and up the outside stairs to the ballroom
which is now their chapel
and also, for one moment each year, the Tomb of Christ.
The knocking at the gate then. Empty! "He is risen."
The bearded one turns about in his blessed amazement
("Christos Basileus—Christ the King is risen!"
Defective loudspeakers gargle in Slavic gutturals)
and blesses us below.
The faithful cross themselves,
the cheap frame of light bulbs tacked up over the courtyard
flares out the miracle: X B

Easter. Faithful and faithless
we light our candles, we of the throng—
one by one, each from his neighbor—
to be held in one hand a few moments, the fire guarded in the curve
    of the other,
while the procession enters rejoicing
the Tomb that has opened, now, to a peopled heaven
where soon the chanting will begin.

I, as always,
take my flame from yours.

From the Kuan-Tzu

East is the time of stars:
its country is the spring.
Winds yield wood and bone
growth, abundance, joy.
Make clean the spirit's places
set house and land in order
plant, cultivate the fields
repair bridges and dams.
Pardon all who have wronged you
make compromises, adjustments
send gifts to those you love
be open in all directions.
Then shall the slow rains fall
and winds blow softly their promise
of calm lives attaining ripe age,
of animals waxing and thriving.

South is the time of the sun:
its land is the land of summer.
Fire shapes pure act
rejoicing in its sufficiency
consumed in very being
as free gift and enjoyment.
Pause then, take your pleasure
in the self's proud assertion
life's long-stayed fruitions
love and love's diversions.

West is the time of the zodiac:
its country is the autumn.
Metal deep in earth
sends forth its glint of sadness
nails and horns and antlers
severity and silence.
Search yourself within
keen-set against all laxness,

dare not be dissolute
strictly seek uprightness.

North is the time of the moon:
its country is the winter.
Water inures to ice,
snow scatters on meadow,
cold nourishes rich blood
with flares of mild anger.
Hope scatters in darkness
but blood moves powerfully:
seek purity within
store up in secrecy.

At center stands the earth:
its country is for ever.
It gives each season in turn
the strength that makes it stable.
Friend of the wind and rain
impartial, correct
it builds the flesh of bodies
and gives this breathing world
harmony and poise
from which to live the changes.

The Step

From where you are at any moment you
may step off into death.
Is it not a clinching thought?
I do not mean a stoical bravado
of making the great decision blade in hand
but the awareness, all so simple, that
right in the middle of the day
you may be called to an adjoining room.

from

DEATH MOTHER AND OTHER POEMS

(1979)

"Death's dreadful advent is the mark of man,
And ev'ry thought that misses it is blind."

I

Canandaigua

Lake of green—
   those mornings in Canandaigua
I'd wake up on the sleeping-porch
with kittens walking all over me
tails up, purring... We
had five or six from one litter:
their bodies wove softly through our hands
and the children gave each one a name.
Came mid-August,
you crushed one under the car one day
starting up in a hurry,
and had five old-fashioneds for supper and cried all night.
At the end of summer we gave the rest back to a farmer.

Lake of green—
   Iroquois dawns—
I read Francis Parkman,
and Doktor Faustus in page proofs,
and after the morning swim
through water transparent and sleek in the buttery sun
sat on the point with a yellow pad
and tried my hand writing poems.
I started fifty or more, I guess,
but didn't finish one.

You wore your hair frizzy that summer.
You swam with your slow easy strokes
the lake you loved as a child,
then sunned yourself on the shore and removed your halter.
You were small and beautiful
and a hater of life always,
retaining in every word and act
a bitterness far too precious for you to surrender it.
And so you read Catholic books
and argued and were at loose ends

and drank down your bourbon old-fashioneds when the dusk came
   on.
You liked to undress in front of an open window
and one night, when the neighbors were having a cookout,
they all walked over to admire the view.

We had visitors—too many,
as people do who haven't made lives for themselves:
the blonde, your school friend, who struck attitudes
all day long in her tight white two-piece Jantzen—
the Village radical in tall cowboy boots
who stopped with his trailer on his way out West—
the "critic" (he later became the admen's adman)
who, rolling his eyes at the hills across our lake,
emitted some bilge about earth navels and Indian totems.

The animals were more interesting.
I found occasional water rats—
self-reliant, a little slimy—
fat groundhogs and lithe otters,
and early one misty morning, lost in the garden,
a half-blind gray-furred mole.
Sometimes, at noon, a fish-hawk circled above us
and far far back in the hills ram-skulls could be found on high
   meadows.

Lake of green—
   late afternoons towards dusk
I'd take the children in the station wagon and drive
halfway back up the hill to the local dump,
and there went our garbage!—sacks, boxes, cans
into a green leafy gulch
as the kids, shouting and laughing,
took turns with me tossing it down.
And we rode home singing songs—
"John Henry" and "Willy the Weeper"
and "I've Been Workin' on the Railroad"—
and had a last swim before supper.

At night cool air drifted in from the lake—
   time for stories. As you sat with your drink,
I read aloud from A. A. Milne
or Oz or *The Wind in the Willows,*
and we'd kiss our dear ones goodnight and tuck them in,
and the evening was ours, it seemed . . .

Not so. Each evening was finally itself.
And ourselves were not ours, perhaps, but part of time's
endless elaborations of nothingness.
The days passed, the summer too,
and then it was over, all over, and we returned
to the city and a larger home in time,
and moved ahead through changing years,
and none of us ever went back to Canandaigua
except you—who are buried now
in the graveyard looking down on the lake from the top of the hill.

Moments

1
White clouds, red leaves flying—
I paddle home across the lake.
Alighting on my bow, a crane perches,
measures me with his golden eye.
(after Shen Chou)

2
At sunset the hills turn purple,
the trees drip still from the afternoon rains.

One can sit alone in the long silence,
sit quietly and sing.

Best of all is having nothing to do:
let the world disperse itself!

A narrow path leads up and around—
nearby, we know, is the home of an immortal.
(after Wen Cheng-ming)

3
A whisper echoes
    from the cloud
above a mountain that is not there . . .
(after Su-Shih)

As It Was

Remember the old peasant of
Broadway and Nineteenth—
scraped red face, a croaking smile and
twisted hands a size or two too large?

Huge-bottomed, she was bulked in swathes of black.
Heaved it all down on a grocer's crate most often—
not far from the corner, in front of the old bank.

I saw her winter evenings on my walks
in sharpest cold, sometimes in snow,
selling puppies from a big brown basket—
litters gummy-eyed and squeaking—
and candy too: gumdrops, licorice
a penny each, and oddly shaped dark cookies
ginger-tasting, dusted white with sugar.

It seemed to me she was old beyond the telling
but she never changed. I was the one who aged.
One day she simply wasn't there any more.

Years later, I thought of her when spring came round
and days grew long again:
how at Easter time she used to sell white rabbits,
and water lilies in mid-June.

The Touch

One may define eternity in various ways—
as contemplation, say, passion or joy—
but preferably not as a blank stretch that runs on and on.
Quality sums it, not extent.

Call it intensification of the actual
to a point at which, cut free from the known web,
it plunges to its depths within yourself:

or, if you like, a process (which seems continuous)
whereby a second world in its reflections
validates the stray tentatives of chance:

or grant it, even, the name of nothingness,
the final staring void on which all other
voids may be visaged as transparent masks:

it touched me at all events this afternoon,
an ordinary afternoon in New York City,
in the eye of the blonde child wearing a dark red tam
who looked at me laughing as I returned her ball—

in the meeting, a few blocks further north on Madison,
with a man who had cried in my room twenty years before—
in the sugary smell from the corner bakery store—

in the dream I ventured, asleep here in my chair,
of eating fruit in a jungle patio:
oranges, strawberries from glass bowls decked with mint—

and yet once more, at the clouded time of dusk
when mind, adrift, moved through its nearer voids
and first the diffident poem showed itself.

The Turtle

In August 1932 it must have been.
The Bering Hill Road, outside of Greenwich, was dirt in those days
with here and there a big boulder poking through.
We eased along it carefully in the Marmon
those late afternoons, near dusk, when we went out searching.

I was ten years old. My mother—young, high-spirited—
loved birds and liked to drive, particularly that svelte old car of hers.
"Come on," she'd say, "let's see if we can find the scarlet tanagers!"—
for we liked the colorful kinds best, though towhees,
dickcissels, cedar waxwings, were all admired in their seasons—

and I'd climb in the front and slam the door, and off we went
out the back lanes and along the dusty Bering Hill Road
and sometimes we saw scarlet tanagers and more often we didn't
but almost always saw something strange and fine:
badgers, orioles, foxes, rose-breasted grosbeaks—once, an eagle.

—This particular afternoon was a hot one, that shimmered,
and we took our drive a bit earlier than usual.
It was a Sunday, I think—I remember the heat-haze
above pale green treetops, and the eddying road-dust.
After going along luckless for a while, we stopped the car

and got out and stretched—and it was then, down the road a ways,
that I saw something dark right out in the middle,
a mottled thing, rounded like a rock, but it had moved.
I ran over, knelt down, and to my joy it was alive!
—a big patient box-turtle, withdrawn into his fortress.

It's hard to describe the love I felt for him,
love, and fear too, in the freshness of wonder
as I touched the smooth hardness of brown patterned carapace
sensing beneath it a life somehow my own.
And then my mother called me to her: a car was coming—

It was an old Model-T with two young men in front.
It came rattling and clattering in a huge cloud of dust
and swerved in its course so as to run over the turtle:
as I watched, the wheel crunched him, he exploded, and the pieces
flew high in the air as they drove away laughing.

"They did it deliberately!" my mother cried out.
No more to be said, we drove home in silence—
but I've sheltered, since then, a certain hard knowledge
that has kept me from yielding spirit or mind
to hopeful assumptions of man's innocence.

"We took a room at the Westbury…"

We took a room at the Westbury
and watched the summer rain pour down
all that long July afternoon …
It steamed in the sheets … At seven o'clock
we moved on down to the bar for drinks.

We sat side by side on the black banquette.
When I touched your arm, you shuddered away
hissing your hate … Still, I could hear
steady outside the cleansing drench.

I let my mind go wandering then
to your litanies of cheap despair,
poor bitch so eager to be damned
(for it seemed you had no use for friends
except as mirrors of your grief)

and all at once, on the second drink
(yourself still festering at my side)
caught sense of something waiting there—

something that seemed fiercely alive
this side the curtains of the rain,
but occupying no certain space:
something that wore my dreaming face …

Madness, a demon, or a god?
These days one can never be sure
or tell, even, the difference.
Whatever it was, *I* made its sense …

What did we do when dinner was over—
go to some third-rate movie or other,
then patch up a truce and head for bed?

That's how it went, as I recall.
In the sparse room we stripped and fucked
and sprawled in the bed-light, hearing the rain—
then, as we lay there lightly touching,
you offered the falsehood of your kiss.

Yes, each accepting the other's lie
we could neither forgive nor be forgiven . . .
But I'm sorry now, poor hateful child,
you found no easier rest that night
with one who awaited what still was hidden.

The Turn

The door of the shed,
      part-way o-
pen, gave out into half-light.

At one side a brown
      paper bag,
half-full of nails, sat crumpled.

The sun had set just
      a minute
or so before, the light was

going fast, the wind
      sifting up
from the shore edged past my head,

leaving at my skin
      its touch of
northern September. Birds on

the move (a few were
      chirping still
outside) would die—so I thought—

thousands, millions in
      emptiness
of passage. How would they not—

those small, precise minds
      fixed on the
one end, not remembering

nests that were cold now?
      And I too
would turn (as red clouds dimmed to

night's all-color) in
      this new can-
niness, sensing how (the mo-

ment of fullness once
      attained) no-
thing remains but withdrawal.

February 11, 1977

to my son John

You died nine years ago today.
I see you still sometimes in dreams
in white track-shirt and shorts, running,
against a drop of tropic green.

It seems to be a meadow, lying
open to early morning sun:
no other person is in view,
a quiet forest waits beyond.

Why do you hurry? What's the need?
Poor eager boy, why can't you see
once and for all you've lost this race
though you run for all eternity?

Your youngest brother's passed you by
at last: he's older now than you—
and all our lives have ramified
in meanings which you never knew.

And yet, your eyes still burn with joy,
your body's splendor never fades—
sometimes I seek to follow you
across the greenness, into the shade

of that great forest in whose depths
houses await and lives are lived,
where you haste in gleeful search of me
bearing a message I must have—

but I, before I change, must bide
the "days of my appointed time,"
and so I age from self to self
while you await me, always young.

II

Orpheus to Eurydice

for Laurence Lieberman

1

As you know, I have not lost you.

It would be presumptuous
in the violet evening
to imagine a freedom
apart from the terrors you have designated,

apart from the body's decay,
the cancer hiving within
and the sullen taste of puke
with which the story ends.

2

Less trade now in this city
which I've loved ever since my childhood's
wintry nights—

but an immense bustle of
decay, as peddlers, jugglers
throng the avenues

and I seek to follow the one
of all these millions
who will hand me your gift—

as it were a flower.

3

Many years have passed since Europe,
dying then as always,
sent me the message shielded
by your green-gray eyes.

I drove you out the back roads—do you remember?
and put my arm across your shoulders
tensed slightly under the white angora.

4
Men are killing men,
they're killing women and children:
whites and yellows are good at it,
blacks and browns catching up fast.
Do you like the touch of blood in your tapestry?

Yes, adored, you do—
and all the more, I expect,
since you can read in their swine-snouts
how ready they are to grovel.

5
Three times I came into you:

in the garden one night of mid-August
when a wind was stirring the shrubs—
on the river's bank while crows were cawing
down a long September afternoon—
and again after the first frost
when the fields had lost their color.

Then you died and rotted.

6
When I went looking for you
the lands were gray and locked:
the straight had been made crooked,
the messages put into code.

It seemed to me, though, that one cold crow I saw
in his uneven passage
from bare tree to bald ground
could riddle me out the answer.

7
And the city was a screen of images
that closed you off
in their virtual past:

the childhood park of games
where we played in my made-up country
falling and scraping our knees—
the soiled room where I encountered women
tangy in the sweat of summer
(you were there, in all those women)
and the first songs came.

8
The smoke of the city at night
rising from obscure chimneys
smirches the moon.
A month after you died
I saw a bat skimming
from the cornice of a public building
and followed his lurching flight above the warehouses . . .

He had no message from you.

9
How to make the descent, then,
to your silent mirror?
The old paths are locked by
history's debris
and we find we dislike the new ones,

their way ever downward
empty of mythologies
with at the end a few bland ghosts
starved to wisps of gesture!

10
And the mystic inner sea
is itself problematic.
I shall find a raft for the crossing, no doubt,
and abandon it on the far side

and making my way through the grey lands
in birdless quiet
attain at the last but a city full
of the shadows of jugglers and peddlers.

11
To find you, to lead you back by the hand,
adored one terrible with claws!
I lust for your haunches
as the old ones lusted for the Sphinx

and am not reconciled
that you be stuffless now
serene in your shadow-pasture
in the last reflex of the mirror—

not reconciled, nor shall be,

12
even though the harsh deaths,
the murders, are continuous
and I do not wish to see the blood
mirrored in your eyes—

even though I well know
you love what is and shall be
and may not by an eyelash swerve
the hand that strikes to kill.

13
But see, now,
your eyes are passageways,
your breasts the memories of fullness,
and those strong legs that clasped me thrice
have walked you into the shadows
from which I say I shall reclaim you
lucidly as though
you bore a second history of my ancient self.

14
What remains—my song?
To be bandied among the jugglers
and parceled out by the peddlers, to be sure.

It is something given as all else is given here—
once in the tangled streaming heap
and once in the mirror.

15
I greet each day as it comes.
May the sun rise and set
with my blessing always
of man and song.
How endless it all is,
how without compunction!

Already I have turned and looked—
and you, already, have been lost again.

III

Samson

When Samson went in unto Delilah
God thundered ineffectually outside.
He could have stopped him in his tracks
but didn't choose to. Was it pride,

or was he just keeping up appearances,
hoping in his heart his champion would fall?
Perhaps he'd had enough of the tiresome exploits
of this bully-boy, forever spoiling for a brawl,

and judging that love, shame and hard times
would make the clown a more interesting friend,
prearranged the razor, the gouged-out eyes,
the enslavement in darkness—and if at the end

he restored for a moment that futile strength
it was only to bring home his lesson of despair—
for when all was suffered and told, the Lord
loved Samson more without his hair.

History

I give you a Caribbean isle of seventy years ago,
a tropic night,
a ship anchored in the bay.
The sailors are drinking rum and thinking about women.

Strumming sounds drift across the water with the scent of hibiscus.
The moon is huge,
but do you not sense the soft
scene's desolation? Of sailors who sadly chat and drink,

of brown-skinned women paddling out in the small boats to trade
        with them,
and of lost homes
cast away in the cold lands
of snowy New England, or Illinois, or Nebraska?

The bodies will mingle, but how may we mingle their histories?
The night is mute,
while far back in his cabin
the captain, who has enjoyed a woman, thinks about hell.

The Trader

"You'll be wanting a woman," Cavanaugh said with a laugh,
"a strong young fellow like you, as soon as possible."
My first day here on the island it was—a hot one—
and he'd been on hand at the waterside when we landed
and seen about having my goods fetched up to the station.
I had from the first a feeling I'd like the place—
the village spread out like a crescent along the beach,
the thatched native houses crouched under sloped brown roofs,
and a crest of forest piling up thick behind.
The station was made of coral—the best house in town.

After he gave me lunch we sat for a while
drinking and getting acquainted on the verandah,
and he told me how glad he was to be going home.
"Twenty years is a damn long time, by God—
I've almost forgotten what Cincinnati looks like—
but you'll find I've left things here in pretty good order."
Then, after giving me tips as to local customs
and the strengths and weaknesses of the chief men in town,
he brought up this sudden business of a woman.

I didn't quite know what to say, so I only mumbled
"Sounds good to me," or something like that. "Why sure,"
he said, "you can have your pick. Come along right now."
And we took a walk through the village, in sunshine and shade,
and wherever we went the brown naked children straggled
behind us, crowing and chirping like so many chickens.
I took closer notice then of the island women:
they seemed right friendly, in their red and blue missionary dresses,
but they were brown—no getting around it—and they ran to fat.

We had almost finished the rounds when I saw to one side
a girl who looked better than the others. She was tall, slim,
with shy pale eyes like a vixen's, and had just come in
from fishing, or so I guessed, because her shirt stuck to her.
"She'll do," I said. "Very good," said Cavanaugh,

"I'll marry you tonight and be on my way tomorrow."
"Marry us?" I asked. "Do you mean you're some kind of parson?"

"Hell no," he answered, "but I keep an old Bible handy,
and I'll fix up a table real nice, covered with white cloth,
and light a few candles, and start reading anywhere at all
loud and dramatic, and it always goes over big.
It ain't legal, that's certain, but these folks don't know any better."

So that's how it was. I was "married" that same night
and left in sole charge next day when Cavanaugh sailed
and had Loana to sleep with and fix my meals.
I reckoned her a pretty good woman right from the start,
better than the run of that lot, because she did her best
to please me, and keep things neat, and had a knack for cooking,
and I didn't have to slap her around more than two or three times
when she started jawing at me while I was trying to think—
she soon caught on that I don't like noise when I'm thinking...

Well—I'd been here only two months, doing very good business
and getting along on the whole just fine with the natives,
when I came down with fever. Oh God, was that a misery!
Three days I burned and was out of my head and raved
and puked up my guts and sweated and stank and babbled
and changed to a boy again chased by filthy brown devils
and felt horrid hell dense and thick all around and inside me.
Then I'd come to myself for a moment and see her face
hanging over me like a dark moon, peaceful and quiet—
sometimes she'd be wiping my head with a moistened cloth,
sometimes it was food she'd be trying to get me to swallow—
I'd see her face through the mist, all dusky and calm,
and I'd have a great thought, which glowed, but then lose it entirely
and sink back again into that stinking swamp.
The last night was the worst. I was trapped in tunnels of ice,
my teeth rattling my skull, and this fear inside me

that I had died, and was dying again in hell.
Oh, I shook so hard I thought I'd be snapping my neck!

It passed in the night. I woke up weak as a baby
with dawn in the room, my head clean-swept and cool,
and a vast soft weight on my body . . . Raising my hands, I fought
        free
of blankets, carpets, scarves, and reams of cloth
that were heaped up in huge drifts to keep me warm.
Then something rustled down on the floor beside me
and slowly raised itself to the morning light.
"Hello," I said. "Are you well?" she said. "Thank God.
I'll go get food now, you lie still right there."
She brought the soup in, helped me get some down
and took a few gulps herself. I could see she was hungry.
"Tell me the truth now," I asked. "How long since you've eaten?"
"Three days. I couldn't swallow while you were sick."
Her words didn't have any special kind of twist to them,
but they made me feel something sudden and strong inside.
"Old lady," I said, "you're almost as good as a Christian!"
—a fool thing to say, in a way, because she *was* a Christian—
I mean, she was a missionary convert like the others
and dressed herself up on Sundays and went to church
and listened to the native preacher and sang hymns,
which was more than I ever did—but I was born one
and she wasn't, and that makes a difference, you can believe me!
Anyway, my saying it pleased her very much.

I had a new feeling for Loana after that.
I always liked her, but now it was that, and different . . .

One day six weeks later I was back in the store checking stock
when I heard her voice sounding out real angry and strong
as if she was quarreling, which wasn't like her at all.
I ran around front—there she was, squared off with a native,
a fat oily brute who was calling her bad names in Kanaka.

"Just a minute," I said, "don't you cuss my old lady that way."
He cut short his yapping and gave me a black, ugly look,
then grabbed her wrist and started to pull her away!
Well, I soon stopped that. He was one of her uncles, it seems,
trying to shame her for setting up house with a white man.

My fist settled him. I may not have broken his jaw,
but it's certain he hasn't been bothering us again.

It's been seven full months, and we're used to each other's ways.
When she looks at me now, she smiles—much more than before—
like she's happy, I guess. But I, I can still see her face
quiet and brown, looking down at me in my swamp.
I found something then, if only I could have held on to it!

You work, you eat, you sleep—the days go by fast—
but when I'm alone in-between times, I've been thinking.
The missionary stops off here every two or three months
making his round of the islands, inspecting his flock.
I don't hold with them much, they're a poor weak sort of man
        mostly,
but I'm thinking next time of asking this one to stay over
and march himself up to the station here at midday.
We'll give him good welcome and pay him a couple of smackers
and have him walk out with the two of us on the verandah—
with the village people standing in a crowd outside,
the men in green wreaths, the women all decked out in flowers,
and sun shining bright and wind blowing clean from the ocean—
and he'll marry me up to Loana right and proper.

In Mexico

Our mood had dissipated: a restless night,
     desires unfulfilled.
I slept on the chaise in the angle of the porch.
When morning came, clear and brilliant,
it brought its usual smells of cooking meat.

I shall do some heads of you in the Aztec sun,
     Serena,
or perhaps, forget it all
this one last glittering day
and bury my head in the fur between your thighs
and fuck, and sleep—
                         letting it all go by
until we go out at dusk to watch the cockfight.

Now a moist wind comes shuddering from the jungle:
what does it know of our moods, our complications?

The sun tells it all.
The sky is cruel.
Call it, if you like, a tragedy—
you leaning there against the whitewashed wall.
Have you not heard me whisper that I love you?

But, see, your lip is quivering:
a tear begins to fall.

Abenaki Poem

To make the deerskin shirt for her husband
first she dipped the skin
in a bucket of strong lye
prepared from wood-ash and hot water:
this made it easier to remove the hair.

She then stretched it out across a square
upright frame of branches tied at the corners
and fastened to poles stuck in the ground.
Squatting before this frame
she scraped the hair from the skin
with a tool fashioned of muskrat bone:
its upper end was secured to a wooden handle,
its lower edge carved into serried teeth.

The skin having been scraped clean, she rubbed it briskly
with brains of the selfsame deer
and smoked it in a thick smudge made from rotten wood:
the shirt could now be counted on
to retain its suppleness
even when drenched by rain or river water . . .

Not much game in the forests of the northeast
that winter (the nights were dark and thick with owls):
a few deer killed, raccoons trapped,
from time to time fish hooked through holes in the ice—
and once a black bear treed and slaughtered.

Counting the children, they were eight in that family.
The men held to the old ways
but she had heard strange whisperings in the north—
and at night as the fire dimmed,
when she had prayed to her manito
and to the evil one abroad by day and by dark,
she added a phrase or two for the new weak god—
the anxious one who dangled from her neck.

The Promise

A million souls wandered out at midnight
into the Great American Nature Theatre,
a scooped-out place beneath Arizona stars.

Many held hands, all looked alike:
they had eaten their suppers of roadside meat,
the daily drug was bubbling in their ears.

In groups, intermingling, they drifted about
emitting their little shrieks of recognition
and exchanging such thoughts as they had during the day.

"I had this nice thought," one of them would say,
"of how we are so much better off than the old ones—
because none of them knew what they were going to do

night after night after night until they died,
whereas we, my dears, are always assured,
each possessing the rest and all being of one mind."

"A lovely thought," the others would reply,
and kiss him solemnly—looking into his eyes—
and it became the Thought that was prized that night.

And then the stars went out as though a hand had snuffed them,
a million heads turned upward, and pictures came out in the sky:
billionaires in rocket ships tempting the speed of light,

skiers on Everest, skin-divers off St. Croix,
firing-squads by the Amazon stained red with blood of the slain,
terrorists from Borneo blowing up Notre Dame—

and a voice came down from heaven that calmly explained
what each event meant, and why it was all the same
as what they had seen ten thousand times before . . .

And at the very last, the President's face appeared
huge and pink, and as they all smiled and cheered,
he told them again that all was well,

that America was heaven and there was no hell
(though the rivers were poisoned, the lands burned dry,
the animals dead, and themselves about to die.)

IV

Death Mother

for Hayden Carruth

1

You came as sleep, warily:
when I woke
things had a deep-blue look.

You disguised yourself as night, but
behind the stars
I saw dark flashes of your body.

And as for dreams—
how many you tried me with!
It seems you never weary of your
hopeful grim deceptions

as though I stood in need of such
visions of filth and blood
to move me to acknowledge your
dominion, mother.

2

Lady, when you were born—
frail, blue-veined from the womb
but destined by a god—
the proud man dashed you down.
You died before you lived

yet from the detested corpse
a raging spirit strode up into heaven
and the man fell shuddering
seeing his death at large.

Now in the night sky
with breasts like elephants,
all circleted in moonbeams,
dark-skinned, in your delicate dark skirt
you dance out our black age.

3

Death is the least of things to be feared
because while we are it is not
and when it comes we are not
and so we never meet it at all.

That was a Greek way of avoiding the issue—
which is, that ever since the blood-drenched moment
of primal recognition,
death has lived all times in us
and we in her, commingled,
and not to recognize her is
not to recognize ourselves.

The lovely body is composed of what was dead
and will be dead again. Death
gives us birth, we live in her.

4

I cornered the thief in the garage at dusk.
Small, furry, with quick-darting eyes
he made no sound but watched his chance.

He had none. I took hold of a heavy stick
and when he rushed me, struck him once
and crushed his skull. There on the cement floor
all at once life came to an end.
Out of the nostrils blood was oozing,
the right eye dripped down from its socket.

I felt revulsion at myself and him.
The dog edged up and nosed the body.
Later, in the dark, I dug a quiet grave,
laid him in it and covered it over,
and all was almost as if he had never been.

5

The breasts of the loving mothers flow with milk:
quiet in the streamside grove
they suckle the sacred children.
Sit, rest yourself for a moment in the cool of those trees
for it seems (on such a day) love must prevail.

But the Mother is playful and sportive,
she of the burial grounds:
at nightfall Helen the fair
in paroxysms of change
shrivels, a hag with withered dugs.

Do not think to escape her
by calling her fortunate name!
From her mouth blood pours in a torrent,
her girdle is human hands,
she frees one in a hundred thousand—
the rest she holds to the game.

6

There was no bulldozer handy, so
we shoveled the corpses into the pit—
twenty of us on detail.

I can't remember which month it was, April or May.
The sun was out, a small breeze was blowing as usual.
It meant wading into a complex mass of rot,
they were so many and so putrefied,
with here and there a leg, an arm, a head.
We wore masks, but gagged even so—
several passed out.

Afterwards, where we filled the earth, it bubbled,
and on the march back Kröger said, "My God,

I'd rather die than do that again."
But he didn't die. None of us did, just then.

7
You cast me from your filthy womb
where snails, worms, and leeches grow
and when I've finished out my time
back down your great gorge I'll go
into your black and stinking gut
and crouch there centuries and rot
and be excreted, or reborn—
it's all the same, it's you I'm from,
your stench, your blood, your pain and lust,
your beauty raising up my pride,
your eyes that gleam in murderous jest,
your ancient sluice that I've enjoyed.
How, mother mine, shall I grow free
of you who keep remaking me?

8
Is it useful to have a mythology of death
or handier just to get along with the bare idea,
the barer the better? Such as
a plain black nothingness: easy to think of
like a light going out. Why
get into talk of legends and deities
with all their paraphernalia?

I deny that consolation is the answer.
The greatest consolation (as Epicurus knew)
is the light going out. All notions
of continuance build up in us expectancy—
and *that* is perhaps the answer: life
as lived, responsive to its fiercest surge,
assumes its own indefinite extension . . .

He has not fully lived, Lorenzo de' Medici said,
who has not felt that other life to come—
and yet one must not dwell on it too much
or put on airs. The light goes out for sure

and all the rest is images—in whose mind?

9
One sweltering Sunday afternoon in August,
walking through the back-meadows as was my custom
I grew sleepy, and lay down in a patch of shade
to rest. Drowsed off; and had this dream I can't forget.

I saw a gigantic woman striding toward me
across the fields: glad eyes in a grim face
and crests of huge dark wings that loomed behind her.
She held in one hand a dripping sword, in the other—
dangling from the intermingled hair—
a thousand human heads confused and bunched.
I was the only person left alive,
and as she neared and looked into my eyes
I saw in hers my own self, burning bright.

This frightened me—my heart shook—and I woke.

10
Who will laugh
in coldest glee
when earth darkens once for all?

When graveyard meats
are the only food,
who will eat the dead men's faces?

And who rides free
in the night sky
holding the mirror that holds the world?

Is it not I
deep in the heart,
I who died before I lived?

Black one,
naked dancer on corpses,
with you as Mother
how shall we fear death.

V

The End

Come
this evening
while the snow
is silently evil outside
and the coachman's black-hatted ghost
twirls in bright moonlight frosty mustachios
to the dead place behind the barn
where the Ford's buckled corpse is rusting away
and the children abandoned that heap of broken toys
that will never be repaired, no never in any world,

and celebrate with me the feast of the immaculate destruction
of all the appearances and appurtenances of this life
which seemed for many years a substantial reality
so validly textured of persons places songs
it merited devotion—but which fatally
now, steady as our breathing,
sinks into sacred nothingness
where only one's
other self
remains

The Wrong Side

The moon is partly hidden
by a white cloud drifting over—
and here, on the inside, by a white lace curtain.

You sit at a table with candles:
two red, one gray.
Your shaded face turns downward as you speak.

"Tell me," you ask softly,
"did he know that you were covering?
If so, I fear he must die.
Think carefully, please, before you reply."

The answer is plain enough
but I pause, and I listen to the wind
coldly shuffling through bare clumps of shrub.

"He must have known," I say,
"to have mailed Gerard that letter.
There is no other sense to it at all."

Your hand comes up from shadow—
you rest your head on it.
Your eyes close for a moment.
"We must arrange a way."

A servant brings in brandy
and hot spiced tea in glasses.
The curtains stir against the brilliant pane.

"The wrong side of the business,"
I say, glancing at the moon.
I see you smile, reaching for the telephone.

The Ghost

It was night, and the mist
came in from the harbor
of that out-of-date town
that had changed but little since I was a child.

The house looked on the central square
where a streetlamp glowed in the darkness:
my old friend, A. B.,
had given me the key.

No one about but a stray dog running
who swerved at me, then slunk away
as I climbed those stone steps slowly,
watched by blind windows from each side.

At the top I paused, my huge key
exerting strength at the front-door lock—
it grated, gave; I walked on through
to echoings dulled in dankish space

and stood for a while in the dim front hall
breathing old dust, letting my eyes
calm themselves to that inner dark.
Then I pulled the big door shut.

I wished to let the silence deepen
around me, to become part of it—
as though it might prove friendlier
the more restrained I showed myself.

The lamplight leaked through soiled panes.
Narrowly, I saw a black
doorway gaping to my right
and up ahead steep stairs ascending.

I have you now, I thought. I shall
not let you pass until you bless me.
Followed my torch through the sideward rooms—
found nothing. Started up the stairs . . .

Halfway up my light went out
and I whiffed a foulness drifting down.
I gagged. Something snuffled up there
not far above me. I felt despair,

as though from a sickness long-forgotten
that would kill me yet—then at my ears
a harsh dark whisper: "Be on your way.
Leave me, fool, you may not stay."

I took two more steps all the same
through fog clotting at my face and hair:
the old ghost smelled of earthenware,
I felt his hatred gnawing me.

"Bless me, old rotting sire," I said,
"bless me, and I will let you be."
But he came on faceless with a groan
and as I clutched the icy rail

in a chill rush he brushed me by
and plunging through the hollowed house,
fled moaning into his night . . .

My light came on. I was alone.

President Poem

A President appeared to me in dreams
solemn-seeming as an undertaker
but unpredictable.

I came across him first ten years ago
sitting in the upholstered cave
of an old black Packard town car parked at random
late at night in the porte-cochere at Borderland
before the old house was torn down.
He was on the alert, reading a stack of mail
while the black-capped driver waited onyx-eyed
up front. Slow winds crept through the pines
to where I watched invisibly observant,
and while I watched, two owls flew overhead.
He read his letters in the dark
calmly with a settled look,
one at a time. He had all the time in the world
it seemed—and nothing now or ever would escape him.

Next at an evening gathering—
champagne, décolletage, and all the rest—
we met in someone's mansion in Vienna
(or maybe Paris: Faubourg St. Honoré).
The sleek dark sideboards glowed
with carved decanters glinting candlelight
as half-seen shapes sidled past murmuring
and a tall black man white-tied at the piano
dismembered Liszt in elegant cascades . . .
Then all at once the President stood up
(for a moment resembling Holbein's Thomas More)
and leaving his little group of six or seven,
laughingly led me out onto the terrace
where suddenly the sun blazed full strength . . .

(Two omens—or one real thing, twice seen?
I never asked what the President might mean

but trusted in the climates I encountered
to lend my thought its edge of definition . . .)

I saw him last early in a year of change.
I sat in a huge stadium
packed with the living and the dead
and watched two shadowy armies play at football.
The stakes were high: would dead and living live
for ever in such precincts as I dreamed
or fall for ever through oubliettes of night?
The score was tied . . . And then he came on field
in stiff dark business suit and low black shoes,
stepped back, took a short run, and kicked the goal
after his dim precursors all had failed.

"Lucky black man in my dream..."

for Rosemary Felton

Lucky black man in my dream
drove me up the vast turnpike
in his galactic taxicab:
all through the night we were headed home.

A rabbit's foot hung from the mirror,
an emerald glinted at his ear,
he hummed an easy-going tune—
"Sail on, Dupree, sail on sail on..."

Our voyaging was south to north.
We crossed a gash where Jersey was
and threaded a tiny river town
whose streets were crooked and thick with mist.

Stopped at a bar for a glass of beer.
The place was jammed, they were singing songs,
my daughter was there, quick-stepping with friends—
she danced up and took the black man's hand.

He gave me a wink, and said, "Come along,
the last lap's ahead, not a moment to lose,
we'll make it together before morning comes.
You hadn't a friend, but now you're strong."

Then under the river and huge with speed
we stabbed through the dark like a striking snake
and surfaced in Manhattan easy and free
before a man or a house was awake!

Lucky black man in my dream
drove me through the night-hushed streets
in his dawning taxicab
as the lights changed red to green...

All the lights changed red to green—
we never stopped, we never paused,
but crossed the city we had won
returning to the dream of home.

Three Children Looking over the Edge of the World

They came to the end of the road
and there was a wall across it
of cut stone—not very high.

Two of them boosted the third up
between them, he scrambled to the top
and found it wide enough to sit on easily.
Then he leaned back and gave the others a hand.

One two three in a row they sat there
staring: there was no bottom.
Below them a cliff went down and down for ever

and across from them, facing them, was nothing—
an emptiness that had no other side
and turned their vision back upon itself.

So there wasn't much to do or look at, after all.
One of them told a rhyme, the others chimed in,
and after a little while they swung around
and let themselves back down.

But when their feet touched solid road again
they saw at once they had dropped from the top of the sky
through sun and air and clouds and trees
and that the world was the wall.

The Summit

If you've just once been happy,
you have the right to assume
you're out of the reach of destruction.

I read that somewhere once and
didn't believe it at all
for happiness as I knew it was

only a point, quickly passed,
on the common road that leads
(as far as one can survey it) to

destruction and nowhere else.
What reasoning was this, which
would deny our time as we've lived it

and make us hostages to
assumptions no one has proved?
What can it possibly mean, to say

that those who once were happy
can "bear to die"? I wonder.
Why wouldn't it be all the harder

since they're asked to give up more?
It's those who are sick, wretched,
sunk in pain, and ready to quit—

like my poor friend Costello,
at Hood back in '44,
who screamed so from his hospital bed

he burst a vein in his throat.
Destruction was fine by him . . .
But I've got the argument twisted—

I see it now all at once—
for plain willingness to die
isn't the point. The point is rather

whether, in someone's life, it
may come to pass that the self
reach a place of high vantage from which,

as from a mountain meadow,
future and past recede, and
the road itself lose its meaning. If

so, when the life is resumed,
something is left behind there
(wedded to the high place for ever)

which knows itself as lasting
beyond the self that moves on:
a thing at home in its happiness

as an oak tree is at home
in its own rich-textured shade,
or as an old fish deep in ocean

is at home, flexing his way
effortlessly, without thought . . .
And this thing it is which remains and

remembers itself and time
moving to their destruction
in the self which they seek to rejoin.

from

REFRACTIONS

(1981)

&

SEVEN POEMS BY MALLARMÉ

(1981)

Euripides: *Choral Passage from Hippolytos*

for Richmond Lattimore

I wish I might find a cave
secret beneath the cliffs
where a god would change me to bird—
then I would fly with the flocks
far, far away where the sea breaks
on Adriatic shores,
where the blue Eridanus empties
and the daughters of the Sun
as their father descends beneath the waves
sprinkle those dark-glinting waters
with tears from their amber eyes
in sorrow for Phaëthon.

I would fly to the coast of apples
of which many tales are told,
the far Hesperian shore
where the mighty Lord of ocean
forbids all further voyaging
and marks the sacred limits
of heaven, which Atlas holds.
There the immortal streams
flow fresh by the couch of God
where he lies with his lovely ones—
and earth, the mother of life, yields up
blessings of harvest to enrich
a bliss that never ends.

Catullus: *Carmen v*

Let's live, my Lesbia, and make love,
and all that chatter of old men
so wise in their decrepitude,
forget it!—it's not worth a damn.
Though at each dusk he dies, the sun
will rise, we know, at dawn again,
but we, when our brief day is done,
sink into sleep that has no end.
So kiss me, love, a thousand times,
then a hundred, then a thousand more,
then multiply those kisses till
we've tallied up a dazzling score
and finally lost count. And thus,
since we ourselves can't add it right,
no envious one may injure us
by knowing the sum of our delight.

Catullus: *Carmen xi*

Furius and Aurelius, loyal friends,
who'll follow Catallus even to the world's ends,
whether he journeys to far India's shore
where the eastern wave beats in with echoing roar,
enters Hyrcania and soft Arab lands,
or visits the Scyth and Parthian archer bands
or plains stained by the sevenfold Nile's rich ooze;
or whether, crossing the high Alps, he views
Caesar's memorials: the Rhine, and Gaul,
and the fierce Britons, remotest tribe of all—
good comrades, set to confront all things
with me, whatever chance the gods' will brings,
take but this one short message to my slut,
short but not sweet. Tell her to live and rut
to her heart's content with the studs she holds so tight
three hundred at once between her legs each night,
not loving a single one in honesty
but draining them dry as bone impartially:
but let her not look to find what once she had,
my love, which by her fault has fallen dead—
as at the meadow's edge a flower lies,
touched by the heavy plow as it passed by.

Catullus: *Carmen xli*

Ameana, that banged-out bitch,
charged me ten thousand—a bit too high!
that ugly snub-nosed slut who sleeps
with the bankrupt boob of Formiae.
You family of hers, what's the matter with you?—
call in your friends, and some doctors, too:
the girl's not well—can't she look in the glass
and see for herself the face she has!

Catullus: *Carmen ci*

Travelling many nations, many seas,
I have come to make this offering, dear brother,
here at your grave to leave a final gift
and speak last words, in vain, to your quiet dust:
for you yourself were torn away from me,
poor brother, undeservedly by fortune.
But still—accept these last gifts, this last tribute
tendered in the old way of our fathers—
receive, dear brother, through these tears that flow
now and for ever, my hail and my farewell.

Horace: *Liber iv, Carmen vii*

The snows have melted, the grass renews the fields,
    the trees are green again;
change succeeds change on earth, and now more calmly
    the streams flow past their banks.

Naked, the Nymphs and Graces dance their rounds,
    but the year, the hurried hour
snatching from us each lovely day, give warning: do not hope
    for immortality.

The cold eases to the western wings, spring gives way
    to summer, which in turn must die
when fruit-bearing autumn has achieved the harvest—then
    motionless winter returns.

The moon swift-changing in the sky regains her losses
    but we, when we have fallen
where good Aeneas is, and Ancus and rich Tullus,
    are only dust and shadow.

Who knows whether the gods will add a tomorrow
    to what we have today?
Everything you give your own dear self will be saved
    from grasping hands of your heir.

Once you are dead and over you Minos has uttered
    his notable verdict,
then, Torquatus, not family, nor eloquence, nor goodness
    itself shall bring you back.

Diana may not release her chaste Hippolytus
    from darkness down below,
nor has Theseus strength to burst the chains that bind
    his dear and loyal friend.

The Emperor Hadrian:
"Animula, vagula, blandula..."

Soul, little wandering friend,
companion and guest of the body,
to what regions now are you drifting—
naked and pale and constrained
with no hint of the old repartee!

Asklepiades: *Greek Anthology* (v, 158)

I played once with Hermione, a charming girl
who wore—I swear it!—a many-colored shirt
covered with writing stitched in gold.

The message was: "Love me, and do not ache
that others have me too."

Asklepiades: *Greek Anthology* (vii, 217)

Here lies Archeanassa
the hetaira from Colophon
whose body, aged and wrinkled,
was still Love's throne.

You lovers who knew her youth
in its sweet piercing splendor
and plucked those early blossoms—
through what a flame you passed!

Dante: *"Spesse fiate vegnonmi a la mente..."*

Comes often to my memory
the darkness Love has fixed in me
so that I cry, self-pityingly,
"What other man has lived this through?"

For Love attacks me suddenly,
life's energies abandon me,
one spirit only lives and moves
within, because it speaks of you.

Then I, to save myself, must force
my steps: a pallid, empty thing
I come to you to be made whole,

but when I raise my eyes to yours
my heart is seized with shuddering
that from the bloodstream drives my soul.

Anonymous (Spanish, fifteenth century): *The Prisoner*

It was in May, bright May,
in the long sweltering days
when lovers pay their court
to soft and willing maids:
alone and sad, I lay
locked fast in the deep keep
and never knew the nightfall
nor glad return of day
save for one little bird
who sang to me in the dawn.

A crossbowman came and shot her—
God strike him deaf and blind!

Leconte De Lisle: *In Excelsis*

Swift as the hunting eagle in his course
man rises soaring through the lambent air.
The time-worn earth beneath him shrinks, withdraws.

Rise. Your strong onrush cleaves the clear abyss
in swells of azure lashed by the hot sun.
Below, the globe spins silent in its mists.

Rise. And the fires burn low, sky chills to ice,
a gloomy twilight grips the whole of space.
Rise—rise—and lose yourself in endless night,

blind vacancy—formless, serene, unbounded—
ultimate expiration of all matter
by the great darkness speechlessly surrounded.

What force drives man to seek that primal light
(while all earth's ancient torches gutter out)—
goads him to where the Source flames whole and bright?

On then—from dream to dream, better to best!
Climb up that endless ladder, and tread down
the ancient tombs where old gods lie at rest.

Now meaning ends and agony begins—
darkness, remorse, revulsion from the self,
bitter rejection of the powers within . . .

Where does it shine, that Light? Perhaps in Death.

Baudelaire: *"Je n'ai pas oublié, voisine de la ville..."*

Our little house, I still remember it
at the edge of town, so tranquil and so white;
the plaster goddesses, time-rubbed and dim,
hid in the spindly shrub their naked limbs,
and the late sun, spilling his gorgeous blaze
beyond the pane that broke the sheaf of rays,
seemed like a curious eye to contemplate
our long and silent suppers, pouring out
most lavishly his handsome candle-fire
on the serge curtains and the frugal fare.

Baudelaire: *A Voyage to Cythera*

My heart, like a bird ahover joyously,
circled the rigging, soaring light and free;
beneath a cloudless sky the ship rolled on
like an angel drunk with blazing rays of sun.

What is that black, sad island?—We are told
it's Cythera, famed in songs of old,
trite El Dorado of worn-out roués.
Look, after all, it's but a paltry place.

—Isle of sweet mysteries and festive loves,
above your waters antique Venus moves;
like an aroma, her imperious shade
burdens the soul with love and lassitude.

Green-myrtled island, fair with flowers in bloom,
revered by every nation for all time,
where sighing hearts send up their fervent praises
afloat like incense over beds of roses

or like the ringdove's endless cooing call!
—Cythera now was but a meager soil,
a flinty desert moiled with bitter cries.
And yet, half-glimpsed, a strange shape met my eyes.

It was no temple couched in shady groves
where the young priestess, lover of flowers, moves,
her body fevered by obscure desires,
her robe half opened to the fleeting airs;

no—as we passed, skirting the coast so near
our white-spread sails set all the birds astir—
we saw it loom: a three-branched gibbet, high
and black-etched, like a cypress, on the sky.

Perched on their prey, ferocious birds were mangling
with frenzied thrusts a hanged man, ripe and dangling,
each driving like a tool his filthy beak
all through that rot, in every bleeding crack;

the eyes were holes, and from the ruined gut
across the thighs the heavy bowels poured out,
and crammed with hideous pleasures, peck by peck,
his butchers had quite stripped him of his sex.

Beneath his feet, a pack of four-legged brutes
circled and prowled, with upraised avid snouts;
a larger beast was ramping in the midst
like a hangman flanked by his apprentices.

Child of Cythera, born of so fair a sky,
you suffered these defilements silently:
atonement for your impure rituals
and sins that have forbid you burial.

Ridiculous corpse, I know your pains full well.
At sight of your loose-hanging limbs I felt
the bitter-flowing bile of ancient grief
rise up, like a long puke, against my teeth;

poor unforgotten double, in your presence
I felt each beak-thrust of those stabbing ravens,
and the black panthers' jaws—each rip and gash—
that once took such delight to grind my flesh.

The sky was suave, and level was the sea,
but all seemed blood and bitterness to me
from that time on . . . Yes, in this hateful parable
my heart, as in a heavy shroud, found burial.

On your isle, Venus, I saw but one thing standing,
gallows-emblem from which my shape was hanging . . .
God! give me strength and will to contemplate
heart, body—without loathing, without hate.

Mallarmé: *Sigh*

Toward your brow where an autumn dreams
freckled with russet scatterings—
calm sister—and toward the sky,
far-roving, of your seraph eye
my soul ascends: thus, white and true,
within some melancholy garden
a fountain sights towards the Blue!
—Toward October's softened Blue
that pure and pale in the great pools
mirrors its endless lassitude
and, on dead water where the leaves
wind-strayed in tawny anguish cleave
cold furrows, lets the yellow sun
in one long lingering ray crawl on.

Mallarmé: *Saint*

At the windows harboring
old sandalwood losing its gilt
of her antique lute that sparkled
once with mandola or flute

stands the pallid Saint, displaying
the old volume opened out
where once at vespers and compline
rippled the Magnificat:

at this stained-glass monstrance, brushed
fleetingly of a harp formed by
the Angel in his evening flight
for the finger's delicate ply

which, without old sandalwood
or ancient book, she balances
above the instrument of plumes,
musicians of silences.

Supervielle: *In the Forest*

In the hourless forest
a great tree is cut down.
A vertical emptiness quivers
in shape of a huge stem
near the extended trunk.

Birds, birds, go seek
the places of your nests
in this tall memory—
now, while it murmurs still.

from

NORTHBOOK

(1982)

"And Paradise is between corruptibility
and incorruptibility . . ."

I

The Tree

Rooted in doubt, you
     leaf out to the sun—
your foot is gnawed
     by an undying serpent.

Your hugeness harbors
     a billion selves
as you raise that dense ladder
     from world to world.

On your ultimate wrist
     the eagle perches,
rememberer, while
     the three veiled fates

water your roots
     from the well of conscience
as the still-to-be-wombed
     clutch darkly your boughs.

Odin

You tore out your own right eye, father,
not because it offended you
but to gain what you thought would be ultimate knowledge
from the person who sits at the roots of the world.
That lost eye shines through clear well-water

but in exchange you've found your double,
a second head to parley with
in time's retentive mirror,
a wisdom both your own and other
to instruct you in the perils of yourself.

And so, lavish of illusion, you hatch your plots
as though to delay the closure of the world—
aware the while that when the great show's over
(since gods have homes only where there's no knowledge)
you yourself can do no more than die.

Odin's Song

In pain I hung
on the wind-rocked tree
nine days, nine nights
while autumn deepened,
pierced by the spear
and given to Odin
myself to myself
as the cold came on

None gave me succor
of meat or drink
when I saw deep down
in the second world
black runes of magic,
ghost-engirdled,
clutched them up to me
and fell back screaming

Now your bodies are
forfeit to me
to be stabbed by the spear
and hanged on the Tree
nor shall I spare you
flesh-wrenching pain
poor children who seek
the knowledge that's mine

Heimdall

You are white clean through:
shadows pain you.
You can pinpoint the flea
at a hundred leagues.

Where the glad bridge ends
you keep watch at the brink
lest some polyp of darkness come
shambling up.

None who is stained
or spotted shall pass:
to the end of this time
we'll have clear demarcations

while you, bright god,
stand at one with your deeds . . .
Who thinks to deny you
had best look within.

Freya

To the north, on bright days you may be seen
in your chariot drawn by white cats
moving across the fields, across the sky
blue-robed, your hair gold-streaming.

You do not acknowledge shadows or the grave:
of your thousand lovers you will save some few
according to your sole desire and choice
to live the aftertime with you.

To obtain the immortal necklace you gave over
your body to dwarfs, who used it loathsomely,
but you remained untouched by their disease—
as gold that's steeped in dung will still be gold.

Njord

Where sea meets land
              in shifting sunlight
are ripplings now, withdrawals . . .

Sun on the rock
              through film of water:
glintings, sly dissuasions . . .

God unconcerned
              half yields himself
in salt spray of inlets

and all's refined
              to subtle presence
where, absent, you reside.

Aegir

The gods drift down to drink your brew,
old alderman of the sea;
for weeks on end
they'll argue in your halls
unraveling their sleek expatiations.

Sensitive as they are
and keen in dialectic,
they see this tangled heap of ours—
the clenched dense world of meaning—
more finely than you'll ever know . . .

But still your mumblings drown their clarities.

Ran

Severe lady,
your nets are out.
They are few whom I would bid you spare.

Jormungand

You rest unpleasantly
                on the ocean bottom
sluggish and muddy—
                hungry too, they say.

You go on a long way,
                all the way round, in fact.
When you caught up to your tail-tip
                you clutched it in your jaws:
from time to time you chew on it
                stupidly and sadly.

One has no conception
                of what your thoughts may be:
perhaps a clouded anger
                at knowing yourself alone,
or huge dim nostalgia
                for the time when all was one?

No matter. When you move
                come tidal waves above,
and one fine day you'll have your try
                at swallowing the world.

Thor

You have a big hammer
to solve all your problems with . . .
Effective to a point, but not always apt.

When the time comes for making fine discriminations,
you head for the hills with that thing on your shoulder
looking for giants whose heads you can pound.

You kill the giants.
But more keep turning up
and anyway, the important problems seem to lie elsewhere—
like right back at home, in the gardens of the gods.

It's not easy to find your way through such tangles
and at times you admit you feel wasted . . . Still,
you enjoy your meals, stay cheerful, and make ready for the end.

Frigg

Having already decided to salvage him
you took the shape of the hunted mountain goat
and led him on to your high castle:
when he passed through the glacier's door
and saw you smiling, he fell at once to his knees.

Later, of the various gifts you offered him
he chose the small blue flowers you held in your hand,
and you were well pleased, recognizing your man.
As long as they should bloom, so long would his own life flourish,
you promised—and dropped at his feet the leather bag of seed.

This was your gift of flax . . . When the plants were mature
and the seed-heads had ripened to heaviness,
you came with your maidens down to his small field
and, greeting man and wife,
smilingly showed them how to pull up the flax plants
and steep them in water until the fibers loosened,
which—dried in the sun, then beaten with wooden mallets
and combed out strongly to separate the strands—
could be spun into thread for the weaving of fine linen.

He learned from you all that he needed and no more
and prospered in the unaging meadow
living the life he had once-for-all chosen
joyfully, through placid decades,
until the day when those first subtle blossoms
began at last to fade . . .
Walking out then through a freshness of young plants
he searched the open sky.
"I'll see great Frigg once more before I die,"
he said to himself, "and thank her for my life."

Old and weathered
he set himself to climbing once again
while you in your silence awaited

behind the door of ice
that final meeting you had preordained.
"Enter, good friend, into my joy:
enter the home so cunningly prepared . . ."
Words like these were spoken long ago
even before the man himself was planted—
and now he has arrived . . . High goddess,
tell, if you will, the wonder.
To that lovely cool ecstasy of yours
does his mortality taste fresh and rare?

Tyr

It was because you trusted gods and men
as though all shared your large simplicity
that you put your hand into the foul beast's mouth

and lost it. And so there's an arm hereabouts
without a hand, while in the second world
a strong hand goes about on a shadowy arm
performing righteous deeds (for you sought to be righteous).

You never reflected, but paid the price of purity—
and now that a new word gathers in your head
remote and manifold, as from a mirror,
you find yourself unsure of what may threaten . . .

Speak it out nonetheless! as the dark draws down.

Loki

Having said *no* more times than
the fates can count, you still
maintain that sinuous existence
bearing uneasily on ours.

A difficult love attaches you
to us, like strife,
from the instant the word is spoken
and you come dancing over the threshold
ready to serve or destroy—

for we value your touch of humor,
your willingness to see us through our scrapes,
but recognizing at times behind the laughter
a huge shape sullenly cold,
grimly receding snakelike backward . . .

You're a hater, it seems, after all—and wise,
for nothing is but merits hate
in all this stinking daily clutch
of what we call the human,

nothing but must be denied at last,
Denier, if we would be true—
nothing enduring but death in its changes
masked by the unstable glare—

while the world on its way to fire
trembles at the edge of meaning
as that which sustains it destroys it
in the frail moment's passing . . .

Each day a new sun rises:
and you too are new each day,

ambiguous god whose flame
warming our ancient house
will burn it down in the end.

Loki's Song

Few may see
further forth
than when Odin
meets the Wolf:
so it is written
but I see plain
the great Tree shivering
in my flame

and you soiled creatures
who hindered me
charring to cinder
as I run free
across the earth's
old stunned domains . . .
Pray as you will, I'll
scorch your bones

Balder

You were too beautiful to go on living,
too much of a being of joy
for the present tense of the world:
you had to be put aside, so that
the process of things and meanings might be fulfilled.

And it was your brother, of course, who had to kill you,
sightlessly letting fly the misguided arrow
in sport, beguiled by the demon:
when he knew the truth, he retreated to the darkest
forest of the world, and starved himself to shadow.

The messenger was duly sent below
to negotiate your release
and "nature" wept for you—gods, beasts, and men.
But since there is always one who will not weep,
you must remain in bondage

mute in the clotted house
while here above, this age of iron
endures its last unravelings
awaiting the winter of betrayal
when the dead will rise with unpared nails,

the serpent lurch from undersea
and winds and wolves announce a day of flame
in which sweet flesh shall shrivel.
Ours, that approaching evil—
yours, this drugged suspension in the mirror-world . . .

But after the blaze a newer day will dawn
cool and chaste, and the earth be green again
(or so it's promised) and from the resonant shade
of the great perished Tree a woman and man
walk out once more into the sun—and laugh

to find, in moist green grass
beneath a sky immaculate of pain,
the ancient golden chessmen of the gods.
Then you'll return, they say, in your loveliness,
leading your dark blind brother by the hand.

II

The Murder

When I heard the screaming, I ran back through the woods—
about two hundred yards, I guess—to the clearing.
I was tired—please understand—and somewhat confused,
having no idea what so suddenly could have gone wrong
with my father, whom I'd left five minutes before
standing, smoking his cigar, by the moonlit pond.
You see, I recognized the screams as his . . .

I ran in a daze down the tree-shadowed path
and reaching the open space, stumbled and fell.
The moon was close to full. I'll never forget
how scrambling back to my feet I felt I was caught
in a trap of stillness and light. There were no more cries
and nothing in sight, as it seemed, except moonlit grass
and the glint of moon on the pond
and back in the elm tree's shade something darker than shadow.

I ran over. It was my father. His head had been smashed
and an ooze of blood and brains was soaking the soil.
God! I was numb at first
but then looking down at the corpse felt a rush of hate
so intense, it was almost as if I had killed him myself.
I felt the pain, too—but my hatred burned like a fever,
as though the whole vileness were due to him alone.

How long I stood there stunned I can't rightly tell—
maybe two minutes, maybe ten—and then I remembered
something else I'd seen from the corner of my eye
but paid no heed to at first in my trouble: a blur
almost too vague to be noticed . . . The memory came clear—
It was something gray as a rat, but larger and shapeless,
huddled off on the grass at the edge of the border of trees . . .

So I turned to it. Nothing! Gone . . . Had I only imagined it?
I tell you I hadn't. It was something outside of myself

that came here from nowhere I know when my father was killed.
There is no more that anyone can say without going insane!
I was walking back home, as I've told you, when it all happened,
walking back home looking forward to my bed,
when a person or thing from far off came down to that clearing
and crushed my old father's skull by the light of the moon—
something I never never could have done
although I'll grant I hated the man like death.

His Last Case

To solve the recent brutal bombings
they summoned Inspector Nayland Smith
out of retirement. For twenty-five years
he had been cultivating roses in an out-of-the-way shire,
leaving his old exploits to be whispered into myth

by those who remembered the poisoned earrings
of the Duchess of Lancashire, or those peculiar cakes
into which a royal personage's evil Afghan chef
had mixed mind-destroying drugs. "Smith, for all of our sakes
you must return to duty," the telegram read,

and the old man obeyed. Back in his dark office,
in a closet to which he alone had kept the key,
he found his black trunk full of multiple disguises
which he donned one after the other, cannily,
as he worked his patient way into the terrorist cells

like a subtle illness. He was gun-runner one week,
crooked financier the next, renegade priest the third,
infiltrating craftily the innermost councils
of the People's Select Committee for the Glorious Revolution
until he had identified each hidden enemy.

A year passed. The stage was set—
the ringleaders converging on a mansion in Belgravia
which Smith had wired in secret. Across the way
he watched sardonically from a shaded window,
waiting till his dozen fish had swum into his net.

It had just stopped raining. The cool quiet street
glistened with moisture as a cab whirled by
and two yellow-slickered children moved with hurrying feet
down the deserted pavement. They laughed in lilting tones
and Smith, for one moment, felt betrayed and alone . . .

It was time. He gave the signal. "Show no mercy," he said,
"for the killers have shown none . . ." His men took heed,
    and when their work was finished, the Committee was defunct.
    Remained only the obliteration of each treacherous cell,
    the gathering in of accomplices and packing them off to jail,

and another brilliant victory was proclaimed by the press!
Smith received distinguished honors from a grateful Crown
and went back into retirement at the height of his renown—
but is said to have confided to one or two close friends
that he'll not return to duty when the bombing next begins.

Captain Blaze

He told me to come around midnight, unobserved,
by the back way through the garden—so I parked the car
off the ocean side of the road, a little way down,
and walked twenty yards through the fog to his gray stone wall.
I saw no one else on foot, no cars, no lights.

That tall gate of white ash—all covered with pictures
he'd carved himself, of Pacific deities—
had been left unlatched as he'd promised: it made no sound
as I passed on through it and up the long flagstone path
between flower beds damply swept by billowing fog.

... You never knew him? I think no one knew him well,
and of course he had no friends: they were long since dead.
He was tall and stooped, very old but very strong,
leather-skinned, white-haired, clean-shaven, with yellowish eyes
(from atabrine maybe? He had sailed many years in the tropics)

and a fixed evil grin. But perhaps you've seen him in town,
moving slow and stately, leaning on a black knotted cane
and all the while wickedly smirking and smacking his lips?
Well, he wanted to consult me on a legal point, he said—
trusted me because I was of old New England stock

like himself, not some goddam dago, mick, or jew,
the new base breed that has sucked all the juice from our land
and rotted our northern strength with its vile weak ways
(those were his words)—it was something to do with his Will.
I admit I was curious: said I'd be over that night ...

There were steps to his kitchen porch. While I paused just outside,
trying to adjust, as it were, to the feel of the place,
I heard a low laugh sounding deep from within the dimness.
It wasn't repeated, but I'm certain I didn't mistake it—
so easy and strong, and full of a dark satisfaction.

I told myself not to be frightened, and went up the steps.
Once again a door gave: I entered and crossed to the kitchen,
a clean empty space dimly lit from its farther end.
"Captain Blaze!" I called out. "I'm here. I've kept to my promise."
No reply—so I moved softly on to where the light shone—

his dining room, I presumed. A single brass lamp
set high on a shelf near some books shed a feeble glow
over massed dark cupboards and chests and a huge oak table
from whose farther shore a seated figure glared . . .
It was he—with a heart-shaking grin on his hideous face.

There were shadows all around, and it seemed as though something
    had moved—
which made me at first uncertain of what I was seeing,
of just what it was that confronted me there. Was he breathing?
Would he speak? Was there someone in hiding? It came to me then
he was dead, or caught up in a trance. I didn't dare touch him.

On the table before him were bottles—blue, amber, and purple
in various shapes, twelve in all. Could this be the secret?
Had he drunk himself strangely to death? No—they were bone dry.
What's more, from the cap of each one I found deftly suspended
a small piece of metal hung pendulumwise from a string.

I squinted and stared at them, wondering if here was a clue
to the vestige of movement I'd sensed a moment before
on entering the room: had these little ambiguous nuggets
been swinging, and winking, and ticking their messages up
to that old obscene horror who gloated and laughed in his chair?

Call me insane if you like. I don't care two straws
what word you finally hit on to help yourself through
your awareness of what may be deeper awareness in me—
for it's not very pleasant, I know, to come up against fear
of the kind that compels you to question your sense of yourself!

What had happened, and what was the point? Well may you ask,
but you won't get an answer from me: I can't comprehend it—
except in this sense I've kept of an evil communion
into which I blamelessly stumbled, or rather, was tricked.
—For I have this bad feeling I'm caught now, with lots worse to
    come!

You know all the rest. He was dead, they took him away,
and vandals (they say) burned his house down the very next night.
Because of the corpse's condition, bloat-bellied and dry,
the coroner found he'd been dead at least forty-eight hours.
I mentioned to no one I'd taken his call that same morning.

Omen

A car with ten headless dead bodies in the back
rolled up the slopes of Mt. Cadillac
and launched itself creaking on the stunned August air—
the blood from its axles dripped red and rare.

Night fell. The car jaunted black among the stars.
The bodies stretched and strutted and made prophecy of wars—
while the ten heads, muttering a lucid speech,
swam the chilly narrows of Frenchman's Reach.

The Skulls

Three human skulls had been tossed into an alley,
        a gritty back alley in Todentown. They were
        brownish-white, pitted. They whispered in the dawn.

"How shall we tell the living ones the truth—the truth
        we know so well? What is, today, the truth we know
        so well? How do we know the living ones will listen?

There is no heaven or hell, so we believe. There is no
        afterlife at all, so we and they believe. Yet here
        we are, whispering.

Are we whispering prose or verse? Things are pretty bad,
        we know, but they're going to get worse. Do the
        living ones feel it in their bones?

There is not an afterlife for real. But we've seen our
        bodies' shadows, passing by. And other shadows too
        at odd times: human beings (as they're called),
        dogs, cats, crocodiles, gorillas . . .

We would like to tell the truth to everyone. We would
        like to tell them how they all must end. We would
        like to tell them how the world and all that's in it
        has to end—

maybe with a gasp or two, likely with a bad smell, the
        whole show slithering into rot . . . That's all there
        is to tell,

and we'd like to shout it to the living ones and make them
        face it! But now and then, we must admit, things seem
        less clear, more complicated

because, you see, here we three are (whatever we are),
    whispering . . . Yes, old bones hang on, it seems—
    what about old thoughts and dreams? Maybe they don't
    give over right away, or not completely—

maybe a mirror right about now would help us see the truth
    more clearly: see ourselves as part of it, see
    mirror-in-itself as part of it—

maybe a mirror is what we need to see ourselves as
    skulls that see—

yes! how we wish someone would toss any old cracked
    mirror back this way: back into this old junky pitiful
    poor excuse for an afterlife, where we don't have
    anything left to do or say

except stare at one another in mild surmise, wondering
    about truth and the holes that were our eyes:
    wondering about that blessed deadly truth we're
    desperate to proclaim

and must be a part of, are surely a part of—because here
    we are, whispering."

III

"I remember the sea when I was six . . ."

I remember the sea when I was six
and ran on wetted sands
that were speckled with shells and the blowholes of clams
bedded secretly down in black muck—

I remember the sun, fishy airs, rotting piers
that reached far out into turquoise waters,
and ladies in white who sprinkled light laughter
from under their parasols . . .

Where was it, that beach whose hot sand I troweled
day after day into my red tin pail?
It's only in dreams now I sense it, unreal,
at the end of an inner road no longer traveled.

Alexander

Alexander cut the knot,
couldn't be bothered to untie it;
he wasn't good at solving riddles,
wouldn't even try it.

His adolescent blade addressed
the ancient hide and pierced clean through it.
Triumphantly he failed the test
and never even knew it.

After

The clouds were moving to the east
that day: I found you lovely
as though all pain were held in hands
that opened and released.

Later I walked outdoors at midnight
down the small-town streets
thinking of hair bleached white with age
and a lion starving in his cage.

Someone was playing the clarinet
softly, behind shutters
through which dull orange light spilled softly
down the gray house-side.

I thought of you between white sheets,
private and alone,
and wondered would I move in your dreams
at all, when I had gone.

Metamorphosis

It was midnight, and cold. From the inn
a few steps behind me came blurred
half-smothered mumblings and clinkings.

I looked down the road. She had gone
but a moment before in her rage,
her hair a hard helmet of gold,

the goddess. She had vowed my destruction,
and what could I do but honor her
still, in her evil whore's guise—

I, who have seen her emerge
naked and suave from the wave
and felt the dense clench of her passion?

Interiorly

Interiorly
the space is opened
unto the god, unto the god it is said

as when I dreamed
of my grandmother standing
in the quiet room at the foot of the stairs

who had risen to greet me
and one other
(the late sun glowing through the long French window)

and who was that other
I knew not then
waking in my bed to the scent of verbena.

Exile

Ovid forlorn by the Black Sea,
old Ezra penned in his cage,
have no more words to offer me
though the green man rage.

By Lac Léman the music stops.
I quail—but from afar
the voice of Basil still resounds:
"Solve et coagula."

Castle Rock

In memoriam Lillian Vissenga

We climbed to the very top that August day
while the others waited below
and time reached back one hundred years.

The immense stone forming the capital of the cone
was bare of soil except in crevices:
overhanging by several feet on every side
the huge earth mound on which it rested,
it had the look of being gravely poised
on its own center—a trifle insecure.
Would our small added weight set it tilting?

No matter—we climbed. Insinuating ourselves
lithely into fissures and over projecting knobs
we worked our way, ascending, around the sides
to the upper surface, a breezy platform
smooth as a tabletop and open to all four points.
Hawks wheeled and screamed from their colonies of nests
on one side of our pedestal,
while down below us little hares were playing
in the ashen furze that thatched the earthy mound
and antelope grazed, far off, on the gray plains.

I dreamed I was my grandfather recalling
the landscape of a lost America—
and took your hand. Hours passed. When we descended,
the sun, declining, bathed the far brown mountains
in a rich amber glow, and deepening shadows
shrouded our patient friends . . . "It's the true end,"
you whispered musingly—and all was silent
as we resumed our memory of the present.

Encounter

I met at noon the white-haired oldster, walking along easily—
loafing along, as he would say it, loafing along easily—
and we both stopped still. "This is a surprise," I said,
"I thought you were dead."

"And so I am," he answered laughing, "dead as anyone can be—
but still I like to wander past the crossroads now and then
where the solid earth I love is joined to the mindscape of a friend—"
he paused, and stroked his beard.

"You're kind," I said. "Never kind," he answered, "only true—and
    truth to tell,
you weren't very likely, but you've turned out pretty well—
a better friend than some who make the claim. So long!" He went
    his way,
his strong back vanishing through the trees.

The Master

When Han Kan was summoned
to the imperial capital
it was suggested he sit at the feet of
the illustrious senior court painter
to learn from him the refinements of the art.

"No, thank you," he replied,
"I shall apprentice myself to the stables."

And he installed himself and his brushes amid the dung and the
    flies,
and studied the horses—their bodies' keen alertness—
eye-sparkle of one, another's sensitive stance,
the way a third moved graceful in his bulk—

and painted at last the emperor's favorite,
the charger named "Nightshining White,"

whose likeness after centuries still dazzles.

"Now that at last I must forego . . ."

Now that at last I must forego
the ocean and its soundings
quietly, quietly
I'll travel only where it suits my fancy . . .

As into blades of grass
moist-green at first dawning
or smudged soiled understones
of crumbled factories at the city's edge:

severe into root and rock
as into anguished love,
urging in dark clarity
this voyage to an inner day that brightens.

IV

Seven Dream Poems

Gawain

Strange, those lighted windows on
an axis running south to north—
their ironies precede us. Now
the night looms vacant like a church
as we walk its floor of hidden lakes
(two comrades in December's dying)
noting no gladder signs of life
than plantlets needing little light . . .

Woman bound steadfast to the earth,
I have hung many shining thoughts on you
in trust you'll gain the realm prepared
for those who risk this winter journey—
while I, responsive to the year,
as fabulous beast with leafy horns
(delightful to think of, is it not?)
subdue my neck to the green chapel.

But first, our vision . . . The radiant Child,
once wrapped in spectral blankets, who
holds out his piece of bread and butter
though earth be mortmained to the snow,
making us know by words unspoken
what the foreshadowed life regains
that grants this weakling world no taste
of its lost elegance and pain—

since he, according to the legend,
long ago was pledged to our aid
he'll not return yet to his senders,
having once crossed to the animal side
(for which my breath shall ever praise him
though it be but a dunghill fume!)—
this Child of the strange heavens is
our child too, Lady, and no blame . . .

Before all else, I trust I'm human:
my head, which I must shortly lose,
signifying imperfect reason,
poor working model of high grace.
Remembrance never will replace it!
but let my painted portrait hang
remorseless in your private chamber
when you're restored to your domain.

The Demonstration

It seemed to be a monk, plausibly disguised
in the tried-and-true attitude of the Dying Gladiator,
who was seeking to propound to me some "ultimate" question . . .

But while I watched, the scene changed again
in this cosmologic handsome picture-show
to a plain country kitchen where a woman's hands
were shaping white flour into pillows of bread
as a mouse walked tiptoe on the faded ceiling.

It cannot be, then, the lie you lie expecting
as a footbridge of remarkable length from hell
that becomes the subject of the demonstration

these days (these nights): no, not by any means,
you cannot play dead in the unspeakable limbo
(spiritual tremors marking out the soul's passage)—

I am not dead but have lain down to rest
in my silent sleepy bunk-room along about twilight:
the outer wall is eight foot thick,
and down on the beach white sand has drifted
negligently into elegant dunes,

and I work a slick witchcraft that yields its beauty
as we suddenly set sail on the antarctic sea
(it is plenty light enough) where the wind sends curling
little pallid waves like lazy whips
while at daybreak a curlew screams out my living word!

I'll not come back—do not wait upon the shore,
kind frivolous women from time's abyss,
do not yield to expectations of what nature may demand

but remember to the last those berries that bloom
purple and russet in your hinterland shades,

the thrush that speaks at nightfall, the stagger-ghost, and the wild Sileni in their caves beneath the mountains.

The Adventure

The very rocks were novel in their mass,
color and stratification,
and the water had the consistency of gum arabic;
when the savages saw the carcass of our white beast
they fled to the uplands with harsh wailing cries.

Innocent of the meanings that were carved
grimly into their isle's black carapace
they killed us all except my double and me.
We had our vengeance later, when
the white estrangement leaked through southward curtains . . .

It whistled, and the whistling drove them mad
so that their black teeth tore their own black flesh—
the while our great canoe,
poleward dividing feverish seas, attained
this emptiness past all conciliation.

The Reflection

Among nighttime tribes, in the nighttime forest,
accusations of witchcraft are leveled against the women:
on the tenth night they learn to turn to jaguars and bats
and are harried to the sky where they enjoy celestial visions.

Out of my six wits with anxiety and grief
for the wanderer lost on my backward shore
I was recognized at once in Schadenland
by one who reached a paw out to pluck my shirt.
He led me to the central hut within a muddy clearing.

A skeleton dangled from the roof's overhang
who began to creak and clatter at my reticent approach.
It seemed he was distempered by the course of these events!
A huff of jungle night-breath proved his sudden ruination . . .

I knocked at the hut door. My companion changing shape
was a gravid insect-thing who bumped the ground and whimpered—
a kind, I thought, to fill my ears at night with slippery eggs
that would crack and leak their venom . . . Turning on the seductress
I spurned her frothy mandibles as the door inched gravely open.

Inside, in firelight, a huge black king
was carving men and women, most delicately, of wood.
They sprang to life unmindful of a ghost's imploring gaze
(it was Rimbaud's played-out doubleganger, dismal and disheveled,
assuming killjoy attitudes behind the black left shoulder)

and walked out past me silently. A shadow sun was sinking
as I strained to see those faces: men, women, a few children—
persons I had known once on the day-shores of ocean—
moving to the darkening wood, comprehending nothing . . .

—Clothe me in jaguar skin, give me secret wings
to ride the difficult air of this sardonic vision

that enunciates a night-sky to a million aching tribes—
but do not ask me, like a luckier man, to propound:

for I reckon from what radiance my revenants have come
(as between eons of night, they say, flash ribbons of perception)
and how they may outlinger every timely shift of shape . . .
Let the dark knowers range at large through moonless hemispheres
and chessmen wander blindly, ignorant of their squares!

Everything that breathes in the origin, is the origin.

The Choice

A clear sky may tell it wrong
when its warming light crosses
eyes and arms of a woman you have loved
and a blue pitcher standing on the window table.

All is bright, and must rejoice
in the sea-light gleaming across to the foothills
as wordless the barley sings outside,
"Think now of November."

Pinned by the exacting sun, the heart
grows its second skin
but always fire has a last word
and speaks it out, no matter—

speaks it out to the troubled ghost
rising at night from a wakeful page
who moves in the shadows of the woman's room
like a man of ash and water.

The ocean girdles this sliding earth
as the hopeful lover chooses,
not knowing what face will be revealed
to a new sun shining through . . .

The woman has a tranquil look
but the room seems gathering in a tear
as he sits in his studious chair all night
reading the breathing book.

From the Terrace

Lucidity of the unredeemed . . .

His presence there below, at a table in the cafe,
wearing as always the pince-nez and bowler hat

distressed us so, one summer afternoon
(as though he were a revenant to be exorcised
from any but the subtlest meditation)

that you and I, becalmed in our own breathing,
dwindled to ghosts of self: when, standing clear,
I suddenly put on his skin like a fiery shirt,
feeling his bones at a great distance inside my chest,

and so ran down that sandy beach at Savanna-del-Mar
to where a beautiful white flag was flying
and a woman's breast rose humming like a beehive
gently from the substance of dreams—

and there resigned all hope of keeping back the dark
(when her hand gleamed white from beside the farthest cypress
beckoning now a night-sky crammed with stars)

until we two had passed beyond this imprecision
back to the terrace, back to moods of sleep

with our quitclaim to the unseen chain of selves.

The Diagrams

The large rains had long since passed in thunder
when I became the subject of a threatening monument
in the old park, by the ocean's edge.

Dismal Sundays! In deliberate stages,
like a pharaoh advancing through the Underkingdom,
I evaded the snares of those excellent sermons

delivered by a mock-man with glittering teeth:
a mother, it seemed, had lost ten sons in battle
and even in dreams breathed their acrid scent.

This was a marvel. But all the while I thought
of you, Clarissima, eyes vivid as moons,
who hold in your depths a thousand melodies

which the fairest landscape may never accommodate:
has the Prince not stared through his diamond lens
all autumn, believing you incapable of folly?

Weighed down by winter now, the ponds are dozing
while five guileful lunatics (impersonating angels)
in worn leather jackets saunter beneath the smoke

of decadent December . . . It's the last fastening
(not that any amount of luck will accomplish it),
the last fascination . . . And farther down the coast

ten thousand wild geese fly in from the north
to the philosopher's cove, and ice begins to gleam
on flashy rivulets, and bacon fries in cottages,

and the women expose their cunts in the cement factory
to idle come-and-goers, to angels with blond wings,
though all afternoon one body is not present . . .

The Image may divide, then, into ghost and lasting bronze,
in different centuries walking the same forest
to the ocean's margin, where an old park awaits—

but I, expectant of the dusk, outlinger these charades
in the moon-eyed progenotrix's hazardous kitchen
(among lightnings elusively aflicker after rain)

and watch a milky she-cat chew the old Book's random pages
as I offer at the hearthside of devious time
these diagrams, homes of the dead.

V

The River

*Nous nous réveillons tous au même
endroit du rêve...*

1

A fresh June morning
    your dress flung across the chair-back
and birds awakening,
released from the book of night.

Here it is, the Day
    like none other from world's beginning
and all we have is in it:
I read you again and again.

2

The sun tells stories
    to the restless river
as the trees listen in.

The river is resistless—
but the trees recall the rain's
lisping insistent voice
urgent at the back of our minds

while the sun tells his stories
    (familiar, widely applauded)
to the river of every day.

3

Two bodies in the river,
yours and mine, moving,
a midday swim. The sun
is sultry and relaxed.

    Have I taken hold of your hand then?
    Is there such sweet ease between us?

It's as though the river sums it all
in our minds and its own.

4

Now you are holding a book:
intelligence there with passion
surviving the individual brain and hand—

and when you speak of it tellingly
as we walk beneath the trees
        a living ghost stirs
in the world where all our thoughts are trees and rivers.

5

Decisions of afternoon: as,
to swim once again in the river
before the day turns dark? or
to read from a book of adventure—
of the kind refused by the crowd?

Whichever, it will be private,
unhandled by the human
except as what is human
may also be river and sun.

6

As the sun dims we begin to think
        of evenings that may have passed by
in the world only the trees know.

Only they know it because
        it's a world deprived of vision
and metaphysical striving,

a voiceless world of dense fabrics.
        You and I holding hands
touch on one corner of it.

7
Sleeping, we boarded a boat
that went drifting through our heads
down dark reflective aisles of
summertime water.

The bitterns and Spanish moss:
a Carolina dream.
Uneasy voices called out, too,
beyond the vegetable islets.

Floating, we were hand in hand,
and when our bed returned
it was as though the book had opened
to our reflective eyes.

8
A voice spoke in the night
        while the stars moved slowly
within our dreaming heads.

Not in ancient thunder, not
in the still small voice of the Lord,
but with something like
the rain's persistent utterance . . .

Insatiable rain!
        Our bodies clasped and clasped.
The weak stars winked out.

9
Morning. A river view
calls out to us obscurely:
you are your naked body, crossing
whitely the open room.

Sunlight tips the trees
as if to say, A beginning.
No more is to be said.

The book lies on the bedside table:
once, it contained the night.

from

NEW POEMS

(1987)

The Christmas Tree

In the quiet house, on a morning of snow,
the child stares at the Christmas Tree.
He wonders what there is to know

behind the tinsel and the glow—
behind what he's been taught to see
in the quiet house, on mornings of snow,

when he's snug indoors with nowhere to go
and mother and father have let him be:
he wonders if there's more to know

about their bright, triumphant show
than he's been told. Is the brave Tree,
so proud in the house on this morning of snow,

all that it seems? He gathers no
assurance from its silent glee
and fears there must be more to know

than one poor child can learn. If so,
what stake may he claim in the mystery?
He stares from the house at the falling snow
and wonders how he'll ever know.

Irvington

In the dawn freshness, when the mists are slowly rising from the
    great lawns and only a few early delivery trucks move silently
    down the lanes,
when the house is quiet but for sounds of deep breathing behind
    closed doors and the subdued creak of your footsteps on the stairs,
to walk out barefoot on the dew-damp grass spotted with clover
    where dragonflies are already hovering and veering, settling now
    and again on the glinting croquet wickets,
across to the garden of four-o'clocks and lupines, of nasturtiums,
    snaps, and marigolds,
pale-hued in muted early night and revealing in the pensive gazing-
    globe their enigmatic presences—

to walk down the gravel drive, stones sharp underfoot, and out
    through the great hedge onto the open road,
to run, feet slapping the tar, for pure joy of feeling the wind rush-
    ing past your heedless frail body,
to feel cotton shirt and shorts light as leaves on the airy child body,
to hear in the distance a screen door slam, a dog bark sharply, a
    woman call out (as you catch fresh whiffs of frying bacon from
    the kitchen of the house across the road),
to look down on the great river far below as it moves slow and strong
    in the early sunlight, hearing the whistle and rattle of the 6:00 a.m.
    train that is just now pulling out of the vine-covered station—

to stop stock-still and close your eyes, remembering the night, its
    mists and derangements,
recalling its shaded ambiguous faces, its paths of fear outside your
    window,
then to breathe cool air in freely, deeply, feeling with each breath
    the self intensify in keenness
as you shout out to the kindling dawn, as you catch up from the
    road's green verge a huge rough rock and hurl it!—

to feel on your forehead the sun's strong touch that greets you at
    the peak of being

sensing it as another self and double of your own—
to be alone, to be glad in aloneness, to be at one with all that
    encompasses you in strength of your aloneness:

to be aware—translucent—as it were for ever—in brightness of that
    opening world . . .

Greenwich 1930s, I

Angie stayed by the victrola
playing "You're the cream in my coffee"
over and over and over.
Burke peered in through the window-panes
from a hawthorn bush outside.

At 7:15 Bill's white-haired mother
turned on the radio—Stan Lomax.
The Cards had topped the Giants again,
one zero, Dean over Hubbell.

Janet was up in the pink room, hovering
pensively between bed and door.
Time to screw before dinner? Hardly,
and anyhow, Van had found her solemn—
"too solemn by half," he'd said at breakfast,
beastly cad with his mouth full of egg!

She'd show him. He wasn't *her* necessity—
but now, God damn it, she'd get her dress on
before that Burke came around from the back
to check the ball scores. What a horror!

Meanwhile, on the living room sofa,
Bill said polite things to his hostess—
reached up a hand to smooth her hair,
then stroked one breast ("you're the salt in my stew")

till Jan came clattering down the stairs.
"I'm here," she called. "Let's eat them pheasants!"
"Peasants, you mean," Bill's mother whispered—

but Angie liked Carl Hubbell's savvy,
the way that southpaw saved his screwball
to fan tough hitters in the clutch:

had little use for Dizzy Dean,
big loudmouth always in the papers . . .

Van and his host sidled in from the terrace
as Bess began announcing dinner
and soon Burke loomed at the folding doors
to say goodnight. "I'll eat with cook."
"Good night, old Burke, sweet dreams!" they chorused.
Sleep with her too, thought Angie as
she took off the record. "I'd be lost without you."

Greenwich 1930s, II

On the porch overlooking the eighteenth green
blind Mrs. Adams rocked back and forth
grinning, and sipping her tea.
Her nurse-companion, white-uniformed,
sucked peppermints beside her.

At the next table: "Isn't she splendid?
Past ninety-one and as mean as can be.
Skewered old Charles on her cane last Monday.
How that nurse stands her, I have no idea."

Shrieks and cheers from the pool, where Roger
Ambler was ducking Ellen O'Neill.
Feeling soft breasts against his forearm
he loosed his hold. The girl slipped free—
then wheeled clean about in a shower of spray
and slapped his head hard with the flat of her hand.
"You God damned lout!" . . . She sputtered, giggling.

My daughters seem happy this afternoon,
thought Mrs. O'Neill beside the En-Tout-Cas
where Susan was rallying with the Rinaldis
and Joe the pro. "Watch your backhand, dear."

"Oh mummy, go away! You make me nervous."
Sue missed an overhead at the net,
but Joe, like a cat, had scrambled behind her
and lobbed the ball deep. "Stay up there," he shouted,
"and cover that alley. Don't let him pass you!"

Meanwhile, fresh chirpings from the porch:
a man in street clothes was walking the fairways!
"He's not carrying clubs, doesn't look like a member—
what's he doing out there all dressed in black?
Call the manager, someone. Quickly!"

No need. It was only the Smythes' chauffeur,
a new one who didn't know the rules
(the word came back ten minutes later).
Mrs. Adams stirred . . . She felt a small chill
as the five o'clock wind came drifting in
from the Sound—and clutched a shawl to her shoulders.
"Come along, dear booby," she hissed to the nurse,
"get me moving. It's time to go home."

Mr. Boyd

"Jesus will take care of it,
my mother used to tell me—
Jesus, Jesus
that's all I ever heard,"

said Mr. Boyd the brakeman
one afternoon near dusk, as
we sat in the slatey clearing back of
Scarborough Station

and looked down at the Hudson where
a few small boats were veering—
"she died eaten up by cancer
with a big sappy smile on her face

still talking about Jesus—
I tell you, kid, it's the cats if
you can just believe in it"
(old Nick the Greek was fishing with

a handline from the dock,
chomping a fat Bull Durham plug
behind his drooped mustaches)
"but *how* can you believe in it—

that's the scramdam question,
with all the things we know these days
or think we know." His eyes
were two brush-covered caverns, as

he squinted far beyond me at
the Hudson and its sails,
scratching beneath one arm-pit
the denim smeared with oil.

1904

The things they did together, no one knew.
It was late June. Behind the old woodshed
wild iris was in blossom, white and blue,
but what those proud ones did there no one knew,
though some suspected there were one or two
who led the others where they would be led.
Years passed—but what they did there no one knew,
those summer children long since safely dead.

Anaktoria

Now that you have made your great renunciation
do you think of us, in our cold city,
those many of us who loved you,
those who have held you close—
do you remember our faces, the touch of our hands and lips?

Something about you had been secured from death,
or so we felt
(fresh, perhaps, from your strong embrace)—
and to watch you while all thoughtlessly you danced
was to share a fierce joy we couldn't quite comprehend.

Now, you move beneath a desert sky
among foreigners, are touched by other hands—
but at night, when the moon rises coldly above our avenues,
we recall old days of triumph
and see you again in our midst:
lean body, candid profile, glittering hair.

The Night Skater

Relishing this health, this singleness,
I reach myself out along the surface of a crystal
that cleaves clear down to my own cold roots.
I am the chill wind, passing . . .

How simple this motion, how free of life and death,
how like a god's in his changing!
It fathoms me: ten thousand stars have scattered
glistenings of midnight all along my veins.

The Body

The body frozen in the lake
      rose up again in spring.
It could not be identified
at first, despite the golden hair,
      despite the ruby ring.

Its finder could not shake the chill
      and suffered sleepless nights
while law and medicine assumed
their harsh assignments, and the press
      performed its squalid rites.

It was the teeth that told the tale:
      a woman from away
who'd said goodbye to the warm Gulf
and placid coasts of pine and scrub
      one bright midsummer day,

and driven north a thousand miles
      to the city on the lake.
Then came six changes of address,
smart clothes, chic nightclubs, and new friends
      whose names could not be traced.

The owner of a roadside inn
      where she and a man had stayed
remembered that long yellow hair
and how she had "the sweetest smile,"
      but sometimes seemed afraid—

and other fragments of her past
      came drifting into view . . .
The finder of the body, though,
felt such strange harrowing within
      he could not see it through,

but left the city on the lake
        before the cold returned.
For twenty years the memory
of that poor body, rising up,
        lurked in his heart and burned,

until she came to him in a dream
        with flowers in her hands
and said, "Forget me, patient friend,
for where I am love has its end,
        and *no one* understands."

Eight Triolets

Leviathan
Leviathan swam on the brimming deep,
a strong-girt island all his own:
little he cared how Job might weep
confronting Yahweh in his deep,
or how the Lord would banish sleep
from desperate eyes that seek his throne.
Leviathan dozed on the ancient deep,
dreaming the Lord was his alone.

1928
The wind blew harsh down Thompson Street
       my first long day of school.
October, 1928:
dead leaves and grit whirled down the street
as I hurried from home on childish feet
fearing to break some unknown rule . . .
Wind whipped dead leaves down Thompson Street—
       and I felt like a fool.

Dialogue
The Tartar horsemen shake their spears
in darkening dreams we've shared, dear friend,
how long now?
         Say, two thousand years.
What goads them so to shake those spears
in fierce disdain of what the years
have taught us is our destined end?
In desperate pain they shake their spears—
for this night's dream reveals no friend.

Katahdin
Climbing Katahdin in 1964
I saw another mountain in the sky,
a monstrous bulk I'd never glimpsed before.

I reached the knife-edge and looked up: once more
that brutal mass loomed down to crush me, for
it had a brow that overhung the sky.
Thus, on Katahdin's peak in '64,
I met the god who taught me I must die.

Two
He was skin-and-bones, she was fat.
     They lived many years together
placidly certain they knew what was what:
she liked skin-and-bones, he liked fat,
and hating the world, gave it back tit for tat
     as they kept close to home in foul weather.
Then the world broke his bones, and she melted her fat,
     and they went down under together.

Adamson
"I have never tried love,"
old Adamson said.
"We've been told that above
all things else, we *must* love—
but when push comes to shove
we want notice instead.
So, I've never known love:
and soon, I'll be dead."

"I'll say goodbye . . ."
I'll say goodbye to the hope of fame,
     goodbye to troubles, too,
and recover the things that are close to home.
If I say goodbye to the hope of fame,
I'll be happy once more in my quiet room
free of the world and its residue.
So goodbye, once for all, to hope and fame!
     (Goodbye to troubles, too.)

"I have been here before..."
I have been here before
      when time stood still:
through the half-opened door,
just as before,
I can see the pale hoar-
frost gleam on the hill.
I have been here before—
      and time stands still.

The Gorge

for Peter A. Brazeau

1

The river in the dream
is best approached at noon
for in the night of the dream
faces that yet might tell
what roads lead up and beyond
obscure the evident stream.

Having passed the sixth milestone
turn right down the second lane
and follow it clear to the end.
No nightshades yet remain to faze
such rigorous hearts as seek.

The banks of the stream, clothed in shrubs,
tumble precipitously
to granite shores that edge a lucid water:
when sun assumes its peak
the bland blaze stills the waves
and perch and trout may be seen

(as an oriole dips overhead)
at ease—hovering, lunging—
above the sun-flecked floor
of mud and mottled stone.

2

Noon is the hour of choice
when the demon's face is masked
and sun attains full glare
(the gorge being gloomy at other times
by reason of its narrowness and
deep density of foliage)—

and noon is the hour of threat.
No vision but must fade

(thus the harsh voice of night would warn
those too-naive who struggle),
nothing but must dissever

into such rags and shades
as mask the claims of being.
No, were it not for the lightsome
play of the circling mind
mirroring what was never seen
from the road that leads up and onward,

there'd be no path to find
beyond this simple stream
that yields itself to darkenings—see!—
as soon as noon be past.

3
What voice is it that speaks
as though from a feast of knowledge
in prose that's dark and supple,
drenched with the pain of sight?
Is it yours, old fond possessor?
Have you found your path to the dream?

The mirrored sun declines
as dawn breaks in the skull
and I see your wiseman's shadow
(impostor sick with love)
in ambush down the glen.

Leave me. Your eyes are closed,
old master of illusion,
to the sacred face that stares behind
this mask of brilliant day.
Leave—but return with each false noon
to glad memorials!

I stay. I hold to silence, dreaming
of those who step beyond the dream—
yet heeding, all the while, this river
that flows unmatched within its bounds.

from

POEMS FOR PAULA

(1995)

"In time all things are seeking completion,
but in *Now* all things are complete."

Words

How shall I say it, dear Paula?
Words may not meet the occasion.
They tend to stray off and lose contact
while love, year by year, builds in silence.

Words are like travelers, troubled
by multiple schemes and arrangements,
sometimes harassed beyond measure,
not certain they'll find satisfaction—

yet all the while trusting that somehow
they'll glean from the zest and disorder
a larger, untrammeled awareness
of what it must mean to be home.

I
Maine

The Hummingbird

This quick one likes to tilt his spear
into each gold and crimson cup
and out again, then whir away
across our garden at midday—
soon to return, and dip and hover,
tasting his favorites once more.

Through the long honeysuckle days
of warm July he'll keep this up.
He starts at dawn. We lie adrowse
in our big bed and hear him come,
mingling his low and vibrant hum
with the soft droning of the bees—

until, one day, he'll disappear
and stay away until next year.
We have no notion of where he goes.
Some day, too, he'll die, and drop
small and stiff to the ground, and rot.
Meanwhile, these hours are his.

August

1

Cicada, harvest-fly,
you come out in the days of the dog:
your males emit the vibrant hum
of timelessness in August fields
now as in those boyhood years
when I believed time had no end.

Imagos imbibe sap of trees;
nymphs live in soil, suck sap from roots,
after seventeen secret years
assume their brief maturity.

2

Ninety degrees of August heat—
the sultriest spell in many a day!
Naked we skirt the beach's edge,
adorn ourselves with seaweed wreaths
and laugh and splash, as though at play—

then ease out through the gentle surge
to cool our bodies in the bay.

3

Via lactea, luminous belt of light
　　"composed of countless worlds,"
your changeless passage calms the ardent night.

Future, present, past are intertwined
within that vast unknowing mind—
yes, in your solemn circuit of a quarter-billion years
　　(one round of the celestial sphere)
you justify this mortal August night.

Nightwatchers

We hear them at first dawn, a small golden ringing that
comes as from many miles away, distorted by distance ... Or
from the innermost coilings of our own ears ... And laughter,
that begins and ends with the sound of wind passing
through leafy branches. Were they in our rooms watching us
while we slept? Or amusing themselves in the moonlight of
our quiet furniture?

Mysterious tunings and tinklings! Do they have bells,
musical instruments? Or do they summon up these sounds
from powers that rest within ourselves? It is, in any case, a
music to which no meaning may be assigned.

Yet it tempts us, with a suggestion of departures.
From our silent rooms, in which (if we could but observe
them at a time when they were totally unobserved) faint
traces of movement might perhaps be detected; from our
sleeping bodies (are we inside or outside them when they
sleep?), out of whose webwork odd anomalies have been
known to emerge; and from the specified, given world—as
when a woman steps away from a mirror and her reflection
disappears.

We think of them as of a multiplicity of individual
entities, in communication with one another, each one per-
haps searching our world for his mortal twin. As the dawn
advances and our windows grow palely bright (our bodies,
too, reasserting their claims to selfhood), these visitors with-
draw. Their chinks and chimes are stilled. Exchanging quick
glances and enigmatic smiles, they retire once again into the
forest of nonbeing.—Shall we ever, we wonder silently, con-
front them face to face?

Out over the bay (in our world) the sun has risen.

Autumn Moments

1

Tonight a smell of brown bread toasting
drifts from our kitchen down to the shore.
A damp breeze stirs as the tide recedes.

West of us, from the ruined dock,
children call out over the water
as one last lobsterman drones by.

It's growing cooler. Hand in hand
we gaze off oceanward beneath
a violet sky that darkens.

2

An old scraped board on the beach at Blue Hill,
pink for six minutes in the autumn dawn,
abandoned, broken, unsecured—
reveals itself as everlasting.

3   (*York Village*)

In the quiet yard behind the Perkins House
this empty, chilly, bright October morning
marigolds glow against a weathered fence:

we hold life cleanly at our fingertips.

II

New York

The Breathing Space

I saw my dear one on the street
walking home with clothes in her arms—
clothes from the cleaners. She rippled along
past where the school was being built

on the next block. I called out to her,
shouting "Paula!" from my window:
shouted twice, three times. A black
construction worker grinned at me

from the unfinished rooftop. Paula
halted, turned, and glanced about—
then, as I called her name once more,
looked up and smiled, and cried "I'm coming!"

Earlier that sharp autumn day
we had phoned the small-town hospital
where an old brave friend lay slowly dying:
her voice slipped ghostlike down the wires . . .

It all gives way to death in the end—
this shifting show of shapes that pass:
that much comes clear as time moves on
and pains outmatch the early joy.

It all gives way in dreams that fade—
and what remains? a whiff, a trace,
some pale residuum of a life
changed now to dust and memory?

That's why I'm grateful for those times
when time itself comes to a stop
on some quite ordinary day,
comes to a stop for a random moment

in which the self gains breathing space
to find itself outside of time—
as I've been found, who still hold fast
that pause made radiant by her smile.

"I love grim autumn days . . ."

I love grim autumn days,
leaves falling yellow, brown
into the rainy gutters
along Fifth Avenue.

Life not so freely ventured
as in glad summertime
but durably maintained:
thus my life has found meaning.

Things yield their uttermost
only in death's conjunction—
I need not tell you this,
dear Paula, you who held
your dying brother's head.

Recall the legend, how
by the murderous ocean's rim
the maiden found, tossed up by the waves,
a simple key of gold—
the only one, it proved, designed to open
every locked door she'd meet with on her journey.

An answer may be given, it seems,
before the question's asked—
a pause outside of time precede
the immutable unwindings.
Death, too, is there with its meaning
before a life begins.

I walk the streets at duskfall
to the room we think of as timeless,
alert to the body's surge,
its doomed and bright defiance—
and climb a quiet staircase
to the mute, unchartered heaven

where lovers, freed from the great wheel,
may reassume their legends.

And so the autumn deepens
till all the leaves are gone.
I hold you close, my dear one:
we lie in bliss together,
in modesty of silence—
while outside our dim window
the darkness settles down.

"I call it back . . ."

I call it back, that cold midnight long past:
dark sky with cloud-shapes, here and there a star,
the air freezing my lungs. I wore no overcoat
as whistling to myself "Blues in the Night"
I crossed the chill quadrangles edged with snow.

I tried to see ahead. What would the years,
so darkly clouded, bring me? First, the war
with all its cruel rituals of loss—
the horror that had overhung my youth
full-blown at last and ready to devour.

But at its distant end, if I survived,
Might I not repossess the life I'd loved?
All ignorant, I thought it possible
and kept the hope clutched tightly through the long
disjunction and distress which I endured.

In vain, of course. The past is past retrieve,
and newer loves and griefs would intervene
dividing me from all I thought I'd known
until it seemed the boy of long ago
had been forsaken with his useless dreams . . .

But just last night, in the dark-lit restaurant,
as candles dimmed and you and I sat musing,
there in the gloom they played that tune again—
and I felt his presence, purged and strangely new,
in this long future suddenly at hand.

First Snow

You have gone your way,
      I'm going mine,
across this newly wakened city—
a city cleansed of memory
whose mutterings are stilled now by the whiteness.

It's separation . . . opening into chance.

I pause: my cheeks
      are bright and chilled.
A woman trudges past. "It's a blizzard!" she shouts.
People are skiing down Fifth Avenue;
Across from me, by the Engineers' Gate,
four laughing children build an enormous snowperson.
A car, half-buried, churns; its tires spin.
—I slog on through the glistening drifts.

At the end of this vast open day, I'm thinking,
when dusk descends and the lights are coming on,
and all is being gently folded in,
      patiently, in silence
our ways will reconverge . . .

I see it now—your brilliant smile of welcome.

New Year's Poem

January days, January days
chillingly on the move . . .

Early morning when all is still
I rest my forehead against the pane
(blanched with rime) and gaze far out
across the city's verticals
which all at once seem cleansed and true.

There's a whiter light in the air these days.
December's glooms have receded
with Christmas and its pangs of loss
as the planet takes a lifeward turn
and all at last is rebeginning . . .

Small clouds drift down the frozen sky.
Along the street rough children cluster, edging their way to school.
An eager jogger, puffy-breath'd, marks time before the stoplight.

New days, and time is on the move—
are we such as can match it?
Stick that old sign up over your bathtub, sweetheart—
the one that says MAKE IT NEW—
and I'll rig mine outside the shower stall.

It's January, the days are opening,
a moment's here to be seized—
and that old Yellow Emperor knew the score:
how life must be reshaped
day by ruthless day
unyieldingly to the end.

Begin. Right now.
We'll wash away the pities of the past
and march on with the days.

The Busses

From our corner window
rainy winter mornings
we watch the yellow school busses
nudging their way down Park
moistly glowing, puddled by the rain.

Stopping at doorways here and there
where children climb aboard
they merge into the traffic's flow
and dwindle from our sight.

We watch—then turn away,
and when in changing light
we look again, we see a stream
dark and serene in China,
down which sleek goldfish dart and gleam.

The Depths

In watered wintry light,
the sleek now easing to rain,
we walk hand in hand, unspeaking,
the streets of this undersea city.

Turning the corner from Park
we have entered the untraveled block
where secretly, four flights above us,
a room and a bed await.

The bed, a strong four-poster
with polished spiral columns,
is Portuguese—carved in the old days
from rosewood, *pao santo*.

Mute in the shaded alcove
it takes note of our coming,
offering now as always
its benison of quiet

and its dreams—of Brazil,
of jungles and canopied treetops
through which the hot sun, thrusting down,
glints and scatters on dark-flowing rivers.

We sleep . . . and awake intertwined
in a room so beset by the dusk,
so peacefully severed from time,
that time itself seems to have altered—

and rise now, and cross to the window
where we stand gazing out through the mist.
Dear companion, we're up from the depths!—
our two sovereign selves reemerging
from all that dark splendor of passion.

The Mermaid

A mermaid's out there, floating
this cool March day, above
soiled, square apartment blocks
I look southward upon . . .

Absurd! What chance these days
of such sweet revelations!
. . . Something, though, with breasts and
flowing hair is sunning herself

right here in our bright New York air
as though she'd just now surfaced
from everyone's unconscious.
Do you suppose she has, my dear,

a thing or two to tell us
of how she will protect those few
who visit her beneath the tides
but can't be coaxed to yield her name?

The Smile

"She walks in beauty," Byron wrote,
who knew the beauty of the real
in women's changes, and the play
of dark and bright their moods reveal.

He knew the sacred game. And I?
Along the way I'd learned it too,
but not its crowning elegance
until that April night with you.

I sat there in my chair, eyes closed,
waiting for the poem to come;
half-dozing, from my depths could hear
your movements in the adjoining room.

Opened my eyes a crack, and saw
you fixing flowers in our green vase:
African daisies fresh from Holland,
purple and red anemones.

Your hands were skilled. Your face, intent
upon that work you do so well,
took on a faint and far-off smile:
that smile told more than poems can tell

of beauty, and the grace of one
at home with her desires and powers.
I treasure it, and always shall—
that smile of yours above the flowers.

Envoi

Go, little book, and make your way
through the broad world as best you may.
I'll not be there to urge you on
or hold you back: you're on your own.

But you, dear Love, who've shared with me
time and events and history,
share now this simple dwelling-place
where timeless, we speak face to face.

from

THE ONE ABIDING

(2003)

"When the soul begins again to mount, it comes not
to something alien but to its very self . . ."
—PLOTINUS

I

Washington Square

Late in the twenties when I was small
in breezy spring and sullen fall
I walked each day to Washington Square
to play with other children there:
      Paul, the minister's son,
      Laura, who loved to run,
Benjamin with his costly toys,
and Sue, who said she hated boys.

Near the north entrance to the park
we'd meet at noon and play till dark
wide-ranging through those endless hours
as though all time and space were ours—
      for when we five combined
      we paid the hours no mind
so dazzled were we by the maze
of wonders opening to our gaze.

Each day that passed revealed a world—
a landscape secretly unfurled
to our five pairs of eyes alone.
As king or queen each ruled his own
      in turn, day after day,
      in strict sequence and sway,
and fixed its boundaries and decreed
the laws which all the rest must heed.

For justice governed all our play:
no single passion might outweigh
the claims of all to equal share
in treasure unforeseen and rare.
      And so we roamed at ease
      through joyful seigneuries
each vassal proven by the sword
loyal to Lady or to Lord.

I still recall those ancient games!—
the talismans, the secret names,
the questing knights and demoiselles
the wizards weaving crafty spells,
    and best of all our fair
      strong fortress-castle, where
tired and exultant, friend by friend,
we met at each adventure's end.

So the weeks passed—until one day
when I arrived at noon to play
near the great Arch, at the usual place,
I found no welcoming form or face:
    no comrade had appeared.
      I waited, watched and feared—
then wandered, aimlessly alone,
up and down those paths of stone.

This was a world, it seemed, this bare
immensity where here and there
dim random shapes loomed into view—
this was the world that strangers knew.
    I, its frailest part,
      received it from the start
as closer to the quick of things
than all our brave imaginings.

I stared straight up at the pale sky
where hulks of cloud went drifting by
and knew myself alone and pure.
"Whatever comes, you shall endure,"
    a voice spoke inwardly,
      a voice not strange to me.
I tracked my hand across my face
and felt the world shift in its place.

Next day all seemed restored. My four
good friends returned—we roamed once more,
releasing brighter energies
as though we'd found new selves to please.
  Thus other months sped by
  and seasons changed, as I,
aware that all must pass away,
lived on intensely day to day.

Comrades!—how has life served you all?
Benjy grew up a drunkard, Paul
was killed in Normandy, and Sue
moved somewhere west, was lost from view.
  Sweet Laura, first to go,
  died of the polio
in '33—my love, aged ten.
Sometimes I wish you back again,

the four of you, just as you were,
triumphant in that eager stir
of childhood—and myself with you
as I was then . . . But it won't do.
  No dream of holding fast
  to a beloved past
can cloud the heads of those who know
what's dead is dead, and rightly so.

Children still play in Washington Square
but they don't roam free, they must beware—
gone is their ancient liberty.
Gone, too, that civic decency
  which cherished old and young
  who shared the common tongue.
America bows to new, weak gods;
its children play against the odds.

Laura, Benjamin, Paul, and Sue,
you've gone your ways. I'm going, too.
Our early joys were dearly bought—
the world was never what we thought—
     and yet, we're justified:
     it wasn't we who lied.
Now leave me, friends, and leaving, bless.
Once more I face the emptiness.

Eleventh Street

Waking at first light in my third-floor room,
I'd wait in bed for morning's earliest sounds:
a cough, a random call, the scraping broom
of the sidewalk sweeper starting on his rounds—

then brightly clear at last from the waking street
the milkman's horse clop-clopping down Fifth,
the milkman's "Whoa!" when he paused at our kitchen gate,
and the big cans clanking softly in his grip

as he went down the steps to our cook's "Good morning, Pete."
"Good morning, Lizzie, you're prettier every day—"
and a moment later he'd hoist himself back on his seat,
give a loud "Geeup!" and they'd clop-clop on their way—

and I'd stretch myself and yawn and scramble from bed
thinking of the endless day that lay ahead.

The Clock

The boy had an odd dream on Christmas Eve.
He went floating through the night in the old hall clock,
now changed into a boat. The moon was up.
A being like himself sat at his side.

His house left far behind, the objects in it
took on with distance strange lives of their own,
secretive and severe. He sensed them there,
holding among themselves dark conversation.

Now there were fields below him, cloaked in white,
with here and there a barn or naked tree.
In burrows deep beneath the snow, he knew,
the speechless animals were warmly bundled.

His double waved a hand, and all at once
the sun blazed out full strength and the world was changed!
A tropic greenness overspread the land,
dotted with fruit trees and bright-blooming flowers.

Behind the beauty, though, a malice lurked—
a hint, it seemed to him, of something shrouded,
not yet revealed, but charged with pain and loss.
Seized with a sudden grief he cried out loud

and saw his semblance shrivel into smoke
as the clock rolled over, dropping him down down
through alternations of the moon and sun
to a place of shadows and ambiguous voices . . .

He woke in his narrow bed to a rainy Christmas.

1932

At Twelfth Street and Fifth Avenue
in front of the old Longchamps
one frigid winter morning, as
I watched for the bus to come,

I saw a dark unshaven man
whose skin was snowy pale
set up a stand at the corner. He
had bright red apples for sale

a nickel each, but no one stopped
to look: they walked on by.
He stood there coatless, shivering,
with a fever in his eye

until a small blonde shape appeared,
a child of three or four,
who came from nowhere I could see—
no one accompanied her.

She wore a blue wool coat, fur-trimmed
to warm her wrists and neck,
fur hat, thick gloves and leggings to block
the cold from every crack—

she ran straight to the tattered man,
hugged him around both knees,
tipped back her head and stared straight up:
I couldn't read her gaze.

And there they stood, she holding fast
as though she'd seized her own,
he making no move to escape
but smiling grimly down . . .

I never saw the end, nor learned
what it was those two might tell.
My bus pulled up, I climbed aboard—
and was on my way to school.

II

May Night

By midnight all the street noises were stilled
except for now and then a slamming door,
a gust of muffled laughter, or—in the distance—
the old Sixth Avenue El's receding roar.

You stood at the window. I had left off playing
Schumann's *Des Abends* on the scratched upright
and turned to you now, thinking at last you'd utter
such words as had eluded us all night.

Your gaze gave back my own. Your pensive eyes,
aglint with tears, darkened as though to warn me
that even now our great game might be lost,

and so I rose, not speaking, and stood by you—
and saw then, on your desk in the dim corner,
that opened letter, vengeful as a ghost.

Dolores

After the night of pain
you did your vanishing act,
Dolores—I didn't see you again
through all that winter of war.

Those "white and heavy limbs"
on which my own would rest
after our lust had run its course
withdrew into the chill

of far New England towns
from which as winter waned
you sent your fitful messages,
obscure and menacing.

"There'll never be an end!"
"I need the pain you bring me."
"I'll come to you once more, and kneel—
and you'll be mine for ever."

Black ink on pale mauve paper—
your bold and spidery hand . . .
the words cut deep as they were meant,
they left a bitter yearning,

yet I withheld reply
and let the pain absorb
trusting that when those wounds had healed
I'd still be unforgiving.

You weren't quite divine,
you see, for all your beauty,
for all that marbled reticence
masking the inner fires—

not yet a perfect idol
despite your cold eyelids
and brazen cruelty of gaze—
no, I could not concede it,

but glimpsed you in my dreams
as a frail puppet-thing
with eyes like dead-bright moons, stumbling
alone down endless vistas . . .

And so when next we met,
one mild midsummer night,
I kissed you once and set you free
in that new wilderness.

September 1957

White sky in the last light.
       Imminence of trees.
Pale birch-clumps amid gray trunks of pine.

Black branchings on the white
       remoteness. Tracework.
Visible clusterings, divisions of leaves.

Pale page of emptiness
       on which some hand had scribbled
a message in impenetrable code—

for years he pondered it:
       how to retrieve it,
how to redeem that last hope and despair.

The Recreant

Voices at evening over the water
echoing or remembered
brought him word of one abiding . . .

Abiding, yes—and unforgiving?
Not yet, he hoped, on this pale evening
washed by damp breezes from the bay—
the tide receding.

What was it that had tempted him
to wander from her pathways?
Glimmer of some false dawn, perhaps,
burning beyond the waves?
The memories, the echoings returned—
all pain and waste for lack of one abiding.

Wasted. Night after night he felt
an insurmountable grief
in all those couplings with soft teasing bodies

as hour by hour her cool voice murmured, "Careful . . .
In the end, you know, I turn my other face."

The Parting

I stood in the pine wood waiting for my friend
by the path along the water—
night falling, one last lobster boat
throbbing in from the bay.
I wished to say farewell, *bonne chance!*
I did not expect to see this man again.

"It's the end, I guess," he said, "but first
I'm glad we can share such a moment.
You've loved this place for years, quite as much as I,
and must surely know what I'm feeling
now that my time has come to leave it behind.
What a heartbreaking sunset! Yes, I'm glad you're with me . . .

Still, you'll agree, I haven't been lucky here,
and maybe this moving on will help me find
whatever it is I've wanted.
I feel like being alone high up in the mountains—
the Rockies, maybe, or Tibet:
I might come upon something like truth—and if I die, so be it."

We watched the swollen sun sink redly seaward
and stood for a time not speaking—then shook hands.
"Goodbye," I said. "Prevail.
May life serve you well while it lasts!
I know you and I will be called as one, in the end."
He smiled . . . I pulled from my hip the flask of brandy
and we each took a sip before he turned and went.

III

"I called up Myrtis from the dead . . ."

I called up Myrtis from the dead
to be my friend and lover.
She placed both hands upon my head
and burned me with a fever,

saying, "Strange man, how can you hope
to make your peace with evil days,
with vermin who infest your land
and soil the beauty of its ways?

Withdraw, and leave them to their filth.
Their illness is not yours to cure
who've drawn your strength from ancient things
and healed your own despair.

Withdraw into the secret life!"
Gently she touched my face—
then faded, leaving me to mourn
and call up Talos in her place.

Actaeon

Actaeon, changed to stag, was ripped
by jaws of ignorant hounds
for having spied the unmentionable
while wandering out of bounds.

And yet, he sinned in innocence
not knowing she was near:
her land had not been posted,
its boundaries were unclear.

It takes a deity, you'll say,
to be so cruel, so unfair!
Too true—but that's the way it works.
At least, he'd seen that Body, bare.

Hypatia

εἰς οὐρανὸν γάρ ἐστι σοῦ τὰ πράγματα

When the vile monks of Nitria
butchered the chaste philosopher
their new God triumphed, so it seemed:
the old ones had forsaken her.

This murder took place years ago,
in March, anno domini 415,
during the holy time of Lent.
Alexandria was the scene.

Hypatia the neoplatonist,
while driving to her school to teach,
was cornered by the filthy swarm
who cursed her for a pagan bitch

and pulled her from her chariot.
The woman was without defense:
she'd scorned the warnings of her friends,
relying on her innocence.

They dragged her to the nearest church
(it seemed the most appropriate place)
and stripped her naked there, and jeered,
howling with glee at her disgrace—

then beat her down to the sacred floor
and hacked the live flesh from her bones
with tiles and shards and oyster shells—
then hoisted high the sad remains

and marched in triumph up and down
the city's colonnaded ways,
shouting the praises of their God
and vengeance on his enemies.

They burned all that was left of her—
last of the great Plotinian line,
Theon's daughter, Synesius's friend,
humbled to dust by Coptic swine.

The bishop who had egged them on,
Cyril (later canonized),
made known to all the outside world
he was displeased, shocked, and mortified

by this excess of righteous zeal.
Still, he kept safe his scurvy crew
by bribing all the magistrates:
he'd have more work for them to do . . .

And that was it. Hypatia died.
The old gods faded past recall.
A new god triumphed—if new he was,
and not the oldest one of all.

In the Private Hospital

At the first touch of dawn I heard the horn-calls, golden and muted,
    far in the distance. They must come, I knew, from the forest—
    from somewhere within that shaded immensity which was
    visible just outside my window

(for I seemed to be lodged at the heart of it) verdant and rustling, and
    extending perhaps for hundreds of miles. Who or what
    was being hunted, I wondered,

and who were the pursuers? The sound drew nearer, then was cut off
    abruptly—and I seemed to hear, from the middle distance, faint
    cries whose sense I could not grasp.

Broad awake, I trembled in bed—between those cool soft sheets
    whose touch had grown familiar during my long convalescence.
    I shook uncontrollably without knowing why,

for was I not secure here, had I not been saved from burning? I was
    whole again and free of pain: surely someone must wish me
    well. I searched my mind for clues to this miraculous healing,

but found I could remember nothing since the night of dread, when I'd
    been torched and left for dead in the old burning city.

—How many weeks or months had passed, and how had I been
    rescued? Those strong hands that had tended me—to whom did
    they belong, what was their motive?

Was the truth by any chance that I had died? Had I donned a new life
    in this altered world? As the day grew silently bright

I could make out, as though seeing them for the first time, the details
    of my neat, airy room: off at my right the white closed door
    (through which, I now remembered, a nurse came and went),
    and along the wall facing me

the few simple articles of furniture—a desk and chair, a table, a small
dresser—all of them polished and new and made of natural
wood—

wood, I could tell, that held the beauty and variety of the forest in its
grain; wood that had been worked by people who understood it—

and near me at my left the window, opening to leafy vastness and
framed by trim white curtains swaying gently in the morning
breeze.

All at once I took heart. "This bliss is real," I thought, "I must retain
it. Whatever my story may prove to be, I must not lose this."
Again a horn sounded,

and in terror I remembered the dream: how at darkest hour of night
my Nurse had come to me and passed her skilled hands up and
down my body,

making me groan in ecstasy and fear. I spent myself, she caressed me.
"Soon you will be well," she had whispered. "Soon you will be
quite ready."

The Tower

From the gray tower in his dream
a chime tolled through the night
putting the maddened birds to flight—

those birds that strayed beyond the dream
into our restless day
and sought the terminus of death,
but never found their way.

IV

The Sign

We came to a low bare hill
and climbed its rocky side,
and found where right at the top
someone had been crucified.

The cross was made of cedar,
its foot wedged deep between stones,
and it canted forward gently
to show off its load of bones.

A short but stocky skeleton
was bound to the unyielding wood
by chains so tightly clenched
they'd hold it there for good—

or so at least it seemed,
for the bones were mostly in place.
I took a step or two forward
to look the thing in its face.

"A short man but a bruiser,"
said Schwartz, after he and Hall
and I had made our inspection.
But was it a man at all?

The rib-cage was intact—
the pelvic structure, too—
the spine had held its place
though ever so slightly skewed,

and the skull remained entire
with lower jaw still hinged.

We all three started and stared at it,
and it stared right back and grinned.

If this was a man, he'd been fashioned
too bulky and thick for his height,
with a head unpleasantly large
and proportions that hadn't come right.

Yes, it looked like a man—but was hateful.
That much came clear to my mind
as I fought off obscure intimations
of something still worse near at hand . . .

"It's an odd kind of ape, I imagine,"
said Hall, "though I'm not really sure,
or maybe a freak, or mutant,
a being that filled them with fear

and blind horror, the people who did this—
who left him to parch and starve
and suffer such ultimate torment.
One wonders what people they were."

"And why on a cross?" muttered Schwartz.
"Did it matter so much how he died?
Was blasphemy what they were after?
And where does the evil reside—

in this hideous sacrificed thing
(and to me it looks evil as sin)
or in those who condemned him?" Well, clearly
Hall and I had no answer for him,

so I only asked, "What to do now?"
"Nothing," said Hall. "Let him be.
Were you thinking of Christian burial!"
Schwartz groaned—and said, "I agree."

It was settled. We'd never reveal it,
this secret so grand and malign.
We descended, resuming our journey,
and left him up there as a Sign.

The Burial

How shall the difficult man
be buried? How indeed?
Who can track the difficult man
or know where he keeps himself hid?

You must catch him first if you can,
making certain he's safe in his box,
then put the whole works in that other—
the one with permanent locks.

Having settled him down once for all
in an absence that's yours to command
you may streamline his speech into scripture
and take all his meanings in hand—

you may smooth out the sense of his riddles
that taxed the dull wits of the tribe,
assign him a throne up in heaven
and yelp the good news far and wide—

but it's useless. Eluding your grasp,
he goes drifting away through the mist
as you stand there clutching the castoffs
from which he implausibly slipped—

and what have you gained for your trouble?
No enlightenment, no guarantee:
just this box which will rot in that other
while the difficult man roams free.

The Shamrock

"I've great days then godawful ones—
I'm in heaven, then deep in the pits—
I try to take them all in stride
without losing my wits

but just can't get the hang of it!"
That's what Tim said one night
in the Shamrock Grill off Lexington.
The bottles were burning bright,

the jukebox aglow as the Clancy Brothers
belted out "Finnigan's Wake"
and I stood at the bar drinking Bushmill's
with Tommy for old times' sake.

"Confucius said that at seventy
he'd 'achieved an unperturbed mind.'
Me now, I'm only sixty-six—
do you think I might still have time?"

It was there at the bar three months later
I had word that Tim was dead,
and downed a last glass in his honor
before walking home to bed.

Recollections of Japan

1

The garden in the hills
shadowy still at dawn
shows no trace of footprints.
And yet, spring has arrived:
the snow is melting patchily.

2

Wild blossoms on the river banks
sway yellow in the rising wind:
see—their images bloom too,
deep in the watery clarities.

3

Warm light floods the countryside.
Summer is all about
and the green takes on a different tone
a shade or two beyond
the green that was here before.

4

A hasty rendez-vous
on the lonely mountain meadow—
our pillows are of grass:
nor shall we ever speak one word
of this our dew-drenched meeting.

5

How long will it endure?
My dear, I cannot tell.
I do not know your heart—
only the intricate tangles of
this dark rich-flowing hair.

6

No moon in the sky tonight.
Is this cold autumn the same
as autumns now gone by?
Though I myself remain,
am I the I I was?

7

What am I then to do
when the harsh winds blow through
this withered trellis?
The leaves are turning brown,
I have nowhere to hide.

8

Through rifts in the night clouds
adrift in winter winds
shafts of bright moonlight pierce
shining remote and cold.

9

And the ruthless winds still blow
at midnight as I wonder—
would I have been thus lonely
home in my own great city?

10

A long year has passed
but this is not what I had hoped for.
The parched fields of summer are
far less arid than
these letters from a withered friend.

Meditation at Sundown

In memory of my son Seth

1

It takes me aback at times,
this slow disease for which
I no longer have a name.

Old names are out of fashion
and the new ones unconvincing:
one suffers nonetheless.

What cure? In the search itself?
In the striving? Don't believe it,
but give the beast his due.

2

From the being born to the dying
life is a butchery.
The primitives got it right
with their ritual compensations.

For those more enlightened, however,
the unacceptable lurks
just beyond the visible circle—
knife at the ready.

3

People dressed in the styles
of the 1880s and '90s
visit me sometimes after dark.

They gaze about my rooms
in their graceful twos and threes
uncertain how to proceed.

They don't like what they see!
I feel it, though they're tactful and
unwilling to give offense.

"Be of good cheer," I tell them.
"Soon I'll be one of you,
  stuffless and serene—

all beauties and contingencies
having drifted safely down
to the place of timeless patchwork."

4
You bear the mark of what you are
as children bear the marks of their abusers.

You do not know just what it is you've done,
nor what was done to you.

Deep in your mind a scumbled mountain rises—
so huge, you'd swear it reaches to the sky!

You sleep, and see in dreams the bridge
on which you may not build.

Black water plays beneath. The span
is brief, the far shore dimmed in mist.

5
Before the great resumption,
a time of fitting anguish.

And the heart is stopped, almost,
in paroxysm of loss
outside the gates that may stay closed for good.

I think of the Chinese masters
in their shacks beneath the moon:
wine and chrysanthemums,
the dignities of exile.

V

The Watcher

I stand here at the crossroads
near the gray strip of beach
among these windblown pines.

Thoughts move through my mind
like clouds through a calm sky—
slower than life, unhurried.

I grant rest to the traveler:
he throws himself down at my feet
and sleeps his way through sorrow.

In grimmest dog-day heat
my ancient fount still brims
with cold unsullied water

while night by moonless night
these two eyes chill as stars
gleam out from the worn mask.

Question not what I am.
Solitary in this place
I lead strange lives elsewhere

and thus am reckoned god:
"god of the rocks and pines"
is how you might conceive it . . .

Worship me then, if you choose,
as one who dreams and waits.
The truth will follow after.

The Priest

Sacrificing
to the four quarters
I find the winds responsive.

The rains come
as the gods decree.
I give thanks and go barefoot, laughing.

How many lives have possessed me—
how many gods have I served?

*

I remember a parching summer
and a voice crying out from a thorn-bush:
it came from the broken skull
of a traveler long ago murdered
whose ghost remained tethered there, raging.
Oh the anger, the pain that consumed me
as our minds intertwined in the heat!

And I think of a year of great snow
when climbing the lavender mountain
I found halfway up a deep cave
in which seven black bears had sought shelter.
Seven—and I made the eighth,
who lingered and dozed one whole season
dreaming my life as a man.

Through how many lives have I traveled,
in how many shapes found my being?

*

Alert now, at ease
in each moment that blossoms and fades
I know myself common as clay
yet all the while kin to the gods,
at home with their vigors and skills.

When I dream, I am one with their dreaming:
their lives come to bear on my own
which long years ago was made ready,
swept clean for the great arrivals.

I was born on the northernmost island,
a woodcutter's only son—
spent my early years sweating and slaving
obedient to my father.

On the day of his death I left home,
went wandering alone through the forest:
learned strength, self-dominion from the black pine,
quietude from the night sky.

Nothing

Nothing, and naked—
thus he confronted the day
mistrusting all motives
but sure of his way.

Released from the past,
he contained it within
as structure and bone
of the men he had been.

At ease in his choices,
knowing evil and good,
might he now bring to focus
what it was he understood?

For he understood *something*,
on his windy plateau,
that quickened his heartbeat
and made his eyes glow.

Rain

Rain, all enduring rain
that afternoon in the country cemetery:
a dripping, placid rain,
a rain intending to stay.

Dull, quiet fields all about us.
A closed horizon.
Tricklings of rain on the gravestones,
the freshening smell of grass.

The dead were there beneath us—
who they had been didn't matter.
Future and past didn't matter,
nor even our own dear selves.

I kissed you on the lips then
(there were raindrops on your forehead)
and you drew your body closer
as we made that moment ours.

"When I awoke at last . . ."

τὴν ἐναντίαν δὲ δραμοῦσα ἥξει
οὐκ εἰς ἄλλο, ἀλλ᾽ εἰς αὑτὴν

When I awoke at last from the desperate dream
a morning mist was drifting off the islands.
I looked down on an empty beach—
saw rocks, saw birds, saw clumps of weed
and the mild waves rolling in.
The song—could I still be hearing it?—still pierced me.

What else did I remember? Shapes of terror,
deep anguish, crazed pursuit.
I groaned, and strove to fight free of it all,
all but that song—voiceless, indeterminate—
which through the dream's long sway had been transcending it
and now, it seemed, survived.
It came, I thought, from a place between sleep and waking.

I rose up then from the grass where I'd been lying
and stretched, and walked about,
and found close by, where the sparse soil edged the rocks,
the ancient image of a threshold god.
He was faceless now and seemingly abandoned—
but I prayed to him nonetheless.

"God of these shores, experienced, enduring—
assayer of all wayward, transient things—
modest master of the moment's chances—
strengthen me, please, for onward voyaging."
As I spoke the words a huge sleep overcame me,
and I dropped to the ground where I stood, and closed my eyes.

Hours later I emerged again from sleep
that seemed unsoiled, untroubled.
I stirred, turned on my side, felt a light breeze,

and opened fresher eyes to the brilliant day.
The sun rode high now and the song had ceased.
From near at hand, through the soft noonday hush,
I heard the gentle scuffling of the waves.

The wonder of the thing came over me:
what was this scene in which I found myself?
I got to my feet again and stared out seaward,
and saw far off beyond the watery dazzle
outlines of other islands, vague and still.
They seemed familiar, yet I could not place them.

I laughed to myself: I was lost.
And yet, being lost, I knew I had somehow arrived
at the place predestined and the time foretold.
The god stood by me still and I bowed to him,
and as I did, all at once the song was resumed—
not voiceless now, but fleshed in human tones.

The breeze blew fresh, and memories returned
of the man I had been in the days before the dream,
and tears poured down my cheeks as the song came closer.
I wept, and knew myself—and then I saw her,
white-robed and tall, walking the beach alone—
alone as every spirit is alone—
head thrown back, "trilling like a swan by Xanthos,"
that girl with splendid tawny hair . . .

After Shen Zhou

A single chime of jade across the waters

as along this rocky shore the moment expands
and somewhere within it is hidden a dwelling apart
to which only the absolute ones make good their escape.

The Way seems not to exist (so the master taught)
and yet it is there—and springtime returns once more,
ageless and unreclaimed, to the inner lands.
What purity! The peach trees are in blossom,
birds chirp and stir, and there by the narrow stream
two white-robed figures wait to greet my crossing . . .

Shall I not make my move at last, and join them?

LAST POEMS

Season of Advent

At the New Year, at the turn of time
my heart turns to its old reckonings.

Season of Advent: memory of a broad street,
oaks and elms, the leaves turning,
the white frame houses still and calm
with the tang of autumn in the smoky air
and here and there a lamp at dusk.
Memory of heaven, or of a lost evening of childhood?
Heaven is future when you're young,
as you grow old it recedes into the past
those last days lived in the pure Moment . . .

Autumn. Long walks past stone-walled fields,
returning at dusk to tea in the parlor
with the kind old English lady. Fearless old age.
So it is in the mind's recollection.
The roads near Princeton keen in the sharp air
in the days of my young manhood, a nostalgia in my heart
for love, for the future, for the mystery of life.

And you, my love, my love of loves,
a child then in the nearby city.
I felt a beauty in the future
but did not see it take your form
till the quarter of a century had passed.
This is the time of your New Year,
love of my life, my tender one,
my joy, my pride, my bread and wine,
body that shelters me, spirit that kindles,
my heart's true friend, my life's companion.

The taste of cold refreshes and makes young.
Let us stay young, then, to our final day,
and then return with gladness to the hands
of Him who brought us forth to love and suffer—
man's beautiful and dreadful destiny.

For now I'm touched by death, and touched, must still
love more and ever more your ways, oh God,
Almighty One I fled from in my youth
Who now, most just and loving, brings me home
on a long road and roundabout, but still
a road I make with your help all my own.
Help me to travel it bravely, gladly, knowing
the roads all end as one in the quiet place
where You have dwelt for ever, in our hearts.

Season of Advent: a prayer and a thanksgiving.
For all of life and time your Word is Love.

Thus at this New Year, turning of my life,
my heart regains its ancient reckonings.

"The scene in the stable . . ."

The scene in the stable
  when Jesus was born
has been widely imagined—
  perhaps, imagined wrong.

Shepherds and angels,
  a star high above,
are pleasant imaginings
  born doubtless of love,

but the person himself
  who emerged from the womb
in the common way
  to the common doom

had no help from such trappings,
  such aids to belief;
he achieved his own life,
  endured his own grief,

a creature of time
  and of circumstance
who grew up into suffering
  and took his chance

and tried his best
  to know evil from good
and shared what he knew
  and did what he could.

The Soldier

In memory of my father

I met a corpse in a forest hollow.
It was a young soldier. His face was green,
his breath gave out a nasty odor,
his eyes weren't what they once had been.

His flesh, his uniform were matted
into the carpet of twigs and mold,
but the four brass buttons still burned dimly
in sunlight that streaked through the branching shade.

I felt like mourning him, but as soon as
I opened my lips to voice my dread
his own slow speech prevented me,
deep-echoing from the ruined head:

"Thank you, friend, for your kind compassion,
but pity is something not to my mind.
Do you pity that rock there, hot in the sunshine,
or the dead tree rotting into the ground?

I'll grant, your pity proves the pain
of the suffering animal within:
take care, though, it not leave you blind
to a few plain truths you'd do well to learn.

Since each poor soul is born to die
and rot, late or soon, in a body like this,
you have small cause—take it all in all—
to mourn my mortal vestiges.

This is not, after all, the boy who laughed
long years ago in childhood play—
nor is it, be certain, the man who writhed
here on these leaves, his jaw torn away—

for I am not I. I have moved on
outside these fastenings of time
past all repair of reason and faith
to the farthest crossing-place of mind:

beyond all ken I have moved on
to the ancient ground of you and me
where drums still beat and banners wave
in last unyielding ecstasy!

—Yet, thank you, friend, for your comradeship.
We'll march together another day
and fight, if we must, in other battles
and still be ready to live and die."

Remember Waco

Remember Waco, the "tourist lodge"?
We drove through fog and got in late;
sweaty, gritty, too tired to eat,
we stripped and threw ourselves down to rest—
and then I held your freckled breasts,
      remember?

We felt around and kissed a while
and said we liked each other's smell,
and then I had you suck my cock—
you tensed at first, as if from shock,
then seemed to like it very well,
      remember?

It was the first time you'd done *that*,
you said, but showed how you were game
by setting to it with a will—
and so, I licked you too, until,
throbbing and quaking, we both came,
      remember?

For half the night we lay half-dead,
then waking hard, I grabbed you tight,
hoisted your ass high off the bed,
rammed in and fucked you like a dog
until we screamed in one delight,
      remember?

Next day: coffee, back to post.
Annabelle Smith—was that your name?—
our acts were scarcely elegant,
but no remorse, no cause for shame
if you or I should that old game
      remember.

Primer

Adam and Eve
their god did grieve
when they took that Bite
in his despite,
so he uttered a Curse
which made things worse
while the Devil grinned
for all had sinned
and must leave then and there
Eden so Fair.

God's dire Gift,
duality,
made Heaven and Hell
realities
while Isaac spared
proved man had learned
god's Judgement might
be overturned
by one who kissed
his rod as King
and Lord of every abject thing.

Thus Man made meek
and merciless
proclaimed great Nature's
nothingness
and left that dismal
Opening
through which his jealous
lord might bring
Punishing Pains
too grim to mention
for those who risked
the untimely Question.

Religion then ruled
in stench and gloom
till Science came
with its new broom,
Technology,
to sweep the room:
swept out the bad,
swept out the good,
till nothing remained
to be Understood.

Vain such cures—
the Void endures:
and the Way may be there,
though not very clear
now that X the unknown
has resumed its throne . . .
youth or old age,
You who turn the page,
my lesson's now done
and yours just begun:

to be man, woman, hero—
as ultimate Zero.

The Voice

Woman's man's angel's
      hesitant
      deathly
the voice of one long dead, it seemed,
or of one who had never lived

spoke the unhouseled words
in Evermore's brave city
softly in the market square
at the heart of the diseased commotion

and all the folk were doomed
      happily
      busily
to long recyclings of the self,
to feckless centuries—

all but one wanderer, who,
having seen the "immortal place,"
cut loose his life in that brief dawn
as once the Buddha taught.

Chloris

Your garden faded, lovely one:
It became the scene of vulgar entertainments.

Fastidious as you are, how could you brook
That squalid rant, those apish mimings?

Was it from simple kindness you withheld
Your deadly counterstroke?—Not likely.
Your kind are all unsparing in the end.

Our kind go stumbling wearily
From dark to deeper darkness
Like blind men burrowing head-down underground.

We failed. And you? You've gone—I don't know where
And can't conceive a place for all that beauty.

You've gone for good, and left us with our losses.

Encounter

He came all muddy out of the river.
Climbed the steep bank thick-plastered in mud
and hauling himself over the edge
lay sprawled on a broad green swathe of grass and tall reeds.

A woman stood near him, naked, in the silence
eyeing him keenly from twenty feet away,
not startled but with a faintly amused expression.
At first he couldn't believe she was there.

He tried to remember his mission—who had sent him?
Slowly stood up. She watched but made no move.
A crow cawed briefly from somewhere close behind him
and all at once he felt the heat of the sun.

He raised one hand above his head palm outward
and took three steps through grass that scraped his thighs.
Her hair was thick and tangled, her body smooth.
When she saw his erection, she gave a wicked grin.

The Thaw

A blazing sun,
slush melting in the streets.
The stories of winter have been told, retold.

At the far end of the city
a prisoner is released
as distant shouts of children
proclaim an ancient joy.

Let the long days advance now
each to its own music,
each to be acknowledged with
due praise and reticence

as through this time of waiting
I think of you, my love:
white blouse, skirt scrolled with flowers . . .
Let this be my new learning.

Bank Street

The Village hussy's oiled nipples
asserted an aggressive charm
advancing through the hangings of bamboo.
In from the window a white lace curtain blew
in a breeze that brought the smells of summer cooking.

Bank Street. Moods and needs were tuned
to perfect pitch that bright June day.
Two lively bodies meeting quite by chance
had swung into the old brisk mating dance
without much thought for how the world was keeping.

"What day's tomorrow?" "Thursday, why?"
"I'm going shopping ... Now, from behind?"
"You betcha ... For what?" "A nice new hat—
if you'll contribute?" "With pleasure." "Good ... hold it now
just like that—
now *harder*, you fucker, oh *Jesus*!" ... And the day declined.

To Nancy

For twenty years or more, dear friend,
You've known the worst and not complained
But held to your calm chosen ways
With elegance and grace.

Courage as a state of mind
Is tending to small things at hand
And this you've done so skillfully
You've taught your friends to see

How subtle textures, muted tones
Give meaning to our tranquil rooms,
How one deft touch of color may
Secure the brilliant day—

And how in life's ambitious weave
Of alternating joy and grief
Even the darkest strands of all
May be made beautiful.

On Madison

"I'm so tired—I'm so *cranky*!"
said the small Korean child
skimming up Madison toward me
hand in hand with her pretty mother.

They came up close in their flowery dresses
sleek and cool, two perfect little persons,
and as they passed each turned her head
and flashed me the self-same smile.

Barbara

It was getting to me bad in '97,
the tendonitis. Petty, unrelenting
I thought it would outlast me.
Told you so at our local pub.

You were sitting as usual at your favorite table
in the back. "How are you, Fred?" you asked,
and I told you I thought I'd maybe never get through it.
"Oh, yes, you will," you said. "Look at me!"

A bad ski injury sometime in the '80s.
Two years recovering, lots of pain, but you'd made it—
and so would I . . . I did, in only one.

You were always there at lunch, alone and cheerful,
a middle-aged woman from somewhere in the neighborhood
who enjoyed museum shows, made frequent trips,
had nieces and nephews you'd visit over the holidays.

We missed you that fall when we came back to the city
and after a couple of weeks inquired of the boss.
You had died in your sleep, he told us, back in June.

No one who worked there knew a lot about you
but somehow or other, a few days after you went
a memorial had been arranged right there in the restaurant.
A dozen friends showed up, with most of the staff.

A good way to go, Barbara.—Still, I wish
you'd been given more time. Strangers have taken your table,
new faces surround me, new lives hem me in . . .
I never even asked for your last name.

"Did you see that blonde we passed back there—"

"Did you see that blonde we passed back there—
nice-looking girl, well dressed and all?
I wait at a green to let her cross.
And do you think she waves or even looks up?
Hell no! Good manners—Civility.
Forget it! They're gone with the wind.

And I'll tell you something else.
Fifty years ago when I was first driving cabs—
it was down on lower Fifth, I think around Twelfth—
I waited at a green in that exact same way
for a tall old lady who'd just started to cross.
She wore gloves, I remember, and a big black hat,
and when she came right up to me, right in front of my cab,
she stopped and smiled at me and made a little bow.
Can you imagine that happening now? I ask you!"

The Garden

Will you walk with me in the garden,
this garden by the sea
where the city ends and the bay begins
and the winds blow free?

Life's clutter is behind us,
if only for a day,
as down these pathways edged with flowers
we lightly thread our way.

Song

Have you ever strolled through Bechuanaland,
Bechuanaland, Bechuanaland—
have you ever strolled through Bechuanaland
in the month of May, my darling?

No, I've never strolled through Bechuanaland,
Bechuanaland, Bechuanaland—
I've never strolled through Bechuanaland,
but I've roamed in between your sheets, dear.

Have you ever climbed Cotopaxi,
Cotopaxi, Cotopaxi—
Have you ever climbed Cotopaxi
on a full-moon night of summer?

No, I've never climbed Cotopaxi,
Cotopaxi, Cotopaxi—
I've never climbed Cotopaxi,
but I've seen you twist in your slumbers.

Have you ever kept watch at the Devil's Hole,
the Devil's Hole, the Devil's Hole—
have you ever kept watch at the Devil's Hole
while the sharks and rays were heaving?

No, I've never kept watch at the Devil's Hole,
the Devil's Hole, the Devil's Hole—
but I've gripped you within me the livelong night
and thrilled to a dead man's breathing.

Alison

Alison, Alison, where have you been?
Off to Bangkok in my dream-machine.

Alison, Alison, what saw you there?
Serpents, pagodas, small men with no hair.

And how did you deal with those elegant men?
I let them handle me now and again.

Did they love your long limbs and delicate shape?
They dressed me in chains like a sacred ape.

Were you mastered? *Yes truly, but felt no regret
to be honored as priestess and sacred pet.*

Alison, Alison, what did befall?
I knew the Three Ways, and cherished them all.

Two Songs

"In Ireland, in Ireland . . ."

In Ireland, in Ireland
where ancient deaths are green
they sing in choir the ancient airs
of gods and kings and queens
and ride in curraghs on blue bays
whose waters sparkle all the day
in gem-stones a fierce queen might wear
along her arms or in her hair
in Ireland, in Ireland
where death is always green

In Ireland, in Ireland
where ancient deaths are green
they dance and drink all day
in a heedless kind of way
as though life held no perils
or pains that they need fear,
as though death never would be coming—
and when night falls at last
they take their dark delight
in the young limber girls
the fine prancing women:
all night they dance and have delight
in one another's appetites
until the sun, returning
renews his ancient light
on Ireland, on Ireland,
where I have never been

"Moses"

Moses went up on the mountain
Moses walked high on the mountain

Holy Moses climbed up that big mountain
to see what he could see.

And what do you think he saw?
What do you think he saw?

The old dark god of the mountain
blood-and-knife god of the mountain
war-and-strife god of the mountain
a-layin' down the law.

Sub Rosa

Your breasts rest softly on my naked chest.
We are alone. I smooth your back and thighs
with gentle palm-strokes now as, breath to breath,
your softness heavy on my naked chest,
we start the ancient game. This is life's best:
in a quiet room, removed from ignorant eyes,
to feel your soft breasts heavy on my chest,
my rod firm-fixed between your steaming thighs.

Tomorrow

She was willing that day,
    had no thought for tomorrow.
She gaily gave way
when I asked her to stay,
all laughter and play
with no foretaste of sorrow.
Not knowing what Fortune
would next send our way,
    we made light of tomorrow.

"A small apple orchard..."

A small apple orchard
had been planted at the river's edge.
I walked there and sat
in the fragrant shade
and watched the river glimmering in the sun.

Pretty soon the dead bodies came floating by.

They came at intervals—
singly, or in twos and threes—
men and women I had known
peacefully, making little disturbance
with peaceful faces set in expressions of finality.

Some I had loved, some not.
Some had been my enemies—
but the world had no meaning on this day of days
as I sat in the orchard
(where a bird whistled softly)
and said my farewells—

and a great peace came over me
in which their voices mingled.

Perfection

He knew he must seek perfection
And prove what the word might mean,
In freedom—not as one constrained
By either hope or anguish.

Since the books of instruction were faulty
And largely discredited
He decided to double the challenge
By working things through for himself.

He had no outer goal in mind,
But rather a state of being—
An identity both close and strange
As much his own as his own right hand . . .

Into which, in the course of years
Of discipline and silence,
He'd easily, suddenly slip
With no one ever the wiser,

Like that Prince of the East he'd once read of
Who roamed through regions of bliss
While his image, intact and serene,
Held sway from the unshaken throne . . .

Meanwhile, he had best come to terms
(he knew it) with life's daily chances:
Should he hatch clever schemes to contain them
Or yield himself up to their ambush?

Prepared though he was for the grapple
With pleasure and pain in their seasons
He found himself putting more trust
In prudence and cool restraint—

For neither in glut nor in emptiness,
It appeared, should one seek satisfaction
Who, recognizing self as other
Has placed his whole being at risk.

Fulfillment must be of the moment:
A matter of rhythm and pacing,
Of contours fittingly shaped,
As private desire came to rest in a world that was shared—

The inner reserve all the while
Maintaining its secret balance
And openness to the unspeakable—
To all the rifts of being.

Acknowledgments

As Frederick Morgan's literary executor, I had considered for several years how best to present a final publication of his poems. I knew that a collected poems was not in order since he had often indicated that certain of his early poems should not be reprinted. All of his drafts and galleys for published books were placed in the Princeton University Library along with his correspondence and his journals dating from 1968 to 2001. What remained were his active files of handwritten drafts on yellow foolscap and other miscellaneous folders along with a three-ring notebook of typed poems with indications on many noting the periodicals in which they first appeared, though few had been published in a book of his own.

With the assistance of two Columbia College student interns, Romy Felsen-Parsons and Isabelle Wilkinson, to whom I am extremely grateful, this material was arranged to determine the finished forms of the remaining poems, which were then typed and placed in an order. According to Fred's custom, these "last poems" were sent for critical appraisal to four trusted poet friends: Dana Gioia, Emily Grosholz, Mark Jarman and David Mason. As a result of their close reading, a few of the poems were eliminated, bringing the final number of uncollected poems to twenty-three. To these friends, I express my gratitude.

While my original thought was to publish a chapbook of these poems, I was persuaded during a conversation with the poet Andrew Motion, for which I am most appreciative, to publish them along with Fred's earlier works, hence this volume, *Epilogue: Selected and Last Poems*. David Mason wrote the excellent introduction, illuminating the poet's entire career, which first appeared as an essay in *The Hudson Review*, Vol. LXXI, No. 4 (Winter 2019).

In preparation for publication, *The Hudson Review* Managing Editor Ron Koury lent his keen editorial eye, Associate Editor Zachary Wood prepared the introduction and a selection of poems for advance appearance in the magazine, and Assistant Editor Eileen Talone was the meticulous proofreader. And my deepest gratitude to the publishers, Kate Gale and Mark E. Cull, the founders of Red Hen Press, whose devotion to poetry brought this book to light.

Grateful acknowledgment is made to the editors of the following publications in which poems in the final section of this book first appeared (sometimes in earlier versions):

The American Scholar: "To Nancy"; *The Formalist*: "Perfection"; *The Hudson Review*: "Barbara," "The scene in the stable . . . ," "Season of Advent," "*A small apple orchard* . . . ," "The Thaw" ("At Large" revised, originally in *The American Scholar*), "The Voice"; *Kayak*: "Remember Waco," "The Soldier"; *Manhattan Poetry Review*: "Bank Street," "On Madison," "Perfection," "Song" ('Moses'), "Sub Rosa"; *The Ontario Review*:

"Song" ("In Ireland, in Ireland . . ."); and *Sewanee Review*: "Chloris," "Primer," "Song" ("Have you ever strolled . . ."). Particular appreciation to Carol Sturm and Doug Wolf of Nadja Press for publishing the handsome limited letterpress edition *Eleven Poems* (1983) that included: "Perfection," "The Soldier," "Two Songs" ("In Ireland, in Ireland . . . ," "Moses"), "Sub Rosa." Also, to W. Thomas Taylor for including "Primer" in the anthology *A Garland for Harry Duncan* (1989).

To Frederick Morgan himself, my deepest devotion for giving me a wonderful life and the gift of his poetry.

—Paula Deitz

Biographical Notes

Frederick Morgan (1922–2004) was a native New Yorker and graduate of Princeton University. During World War II, he served in the Tank Destroyer Corps of the US Army. A founder of *The Hudson Review* in 1947, he edited it for fifty years until the spring of 1998 and remained affiliated with it until his death in his capacity as Founding Editor. His poems appeared in a wide variety of magazines and journals in the United States and abroad. He published eleven books of poems, two collections of prose fables, and two books of translations. In 1984 he was made Chevalier de l'Ordre des Arts et des Lettres by the government of France. In 2001 he was named the winner of the Aiken Taylor Award for poetry.

Morgan spent most of his time in New York City, with summers in Blue Hill, Maine.

Paula Deitz joined *The Hudson Review* in 1967 and succeeded her husband Frederick Morgan as editor in 1998. She is also a cultural critic who writes about art, architecture, and landscape design for newspapers and magazines in the United States and abroad. In addition to her book titled *Of Gardens: Selected Essays*, she edited two Hudson Review anthologies, *Writes of Passage: Coming-of-Age Stories and Memoirs from The Hudson Review* and *Poets Translate Poets: A Hudson Review Anthology*.

Professor Emeritus at The Colorado College and former poet laureate of Colorado, **David Mason** now lives in Tasmania, the island state of Australia. His many books include *Ludlow: A Verse Novel*; *Voices, Places: Essays*; and *The Sound: New and Selected Poems*.